The Ten Commandments

The Ten Commandments

Queenship

PUBLISHING COMPANY

P.O Box 42028 Santa Barbara, CA 93140-2028

(800)647-9882 Fax: (805) 569-3274

The publisher recognizes and accepts that the final authority regarding these apparitions and messages rests with the Holy See of Rome, to whose judgement we willingly submit.

– The Publisher

©1996 Queenship Publishing

Library of Congress Number # 95-072817

Published by:
    Queenship Publishing
    P.O. Box 42028
    Santa Barbara, CA 93140-2028

Printed in the United States of America

ISBN: 1-882972-63-5

CONTENTS

I submit this book, in its entirety, to my spiritual director. If I am in any way contradicting the teachings of Holy Mother, the Church, I regard it as never written.

PROLOGUE

I apologize to the reader for not properly introducing myself, but the Lord Jesus has asked that it be like this.

He has told me: "The purpose of this book is not for you to shine, but for My messages, and those of My most blessed Mother to be known." This is why I am limiting myself to simply transcribing what I believe heaven is telling me.

Things did not happen suddenly. Since 1988, I started to write a series of messages and prayers as if a stronger force than I, sweetly asked me to do so. I would wake up in the middle of the night, and I would write on a small computer. Other times I could not fall asleep, or the messages simply came during the day time. I had started to pray as I wrote. I felt somewhat apprehensive showing God my naked soul.

One day, three years ago, I could not retrieve the writings either through a malfunction of the computer, or because of a mistake of mine. I felt God did not want anyone to know about them.

On November 23, 1992, again I felt God speaking to me, and henceforth His voice became clearer. I felt an increasing urgency to speak with Him. I cannot describe the joy I feel when I am in intimate contact with Him.

THE FIRST COMMANDMENT:
'You Shall Worship The Lord Your God
And Him Only Shall You Serve'[1]
'You Shall Love Your Neighbor as Yourself.'[2]

The Holy Trinity speaks:

"Turn to Me, your Lord, Almighty God the Father, to the Son, King of the Universe, and to the Holy Spirit, the Spirit of Love, the Comforter. Turn to My most blessed Mother, Mary of Nazareth, the Immaculate Virgin who always kept Me company, and who walked through Calvary with her Son, Your God and Your Lord. Do not go further away! Practice and obey My Commandments, because they are the true Law. Stop soiling yourselves with the mundane. It is no longer the time to gather any more riches, nor to live as Herod did. Keep away from fornication, a sin that greatly offends God and My Mother. Be pure and holy like Me, the Supreme Virgin, the Holy of Holies. I serve as your Model, and in My Mother you will find a firm guide who will serve to cleanse your hearts, so that you can reshape yourselves in My Image and Likeness. Look that the End Times will come."

The Virgin Mary speaks:

"Dear children, as I foretold you at La Sallete, the abyss opens here, and here is Darkness' king of kings. Yes, my children, pray for the conversion of sinners, and for your own. I know your frustrations, and your impotence, your sufferings, and your tribulations. I am present in love with every tear that you shed. Remember the poor, those who are in greatest need, and those who thirst for your love. Do not despair. Never turn your backs on the poor because, if you do so today, on the Day of Judgment, my Father will turn His back on you. Do not deserve to be called 'accursed ones' when you hear the words but you do not act on them,

'For I was hungry and you gave me no food, I was thirsty and you gave me no drink... naked and you gave me no clothing, ill and in prison, and you did not care for me.'[3]

Yes, my children, there are so many sins, there is so much indifference, and so much pride in the world. Practise meekness of heart. Now I leave you and bless you in the Name of the Father, of the Son, and of the Holy Spirit."

November 25, 1992 (4:00 p.m.)

The Holy Trinity speaks:

"My little son: these messages are for you, until the right time comes. I am He, the Lord your God, the One and True God, the Holy of Holies. The Most Blessed Trinity, HE WHO IS, WHO WAS, WHO WILL BE, I am Almighty God, the Eternal Father; God the Son, the Redeemer of the World; God the Holy Spirit, Spirit of Love and of Compassion. Never doubt Me.

Today I am comforting you, and I embrace you with all My Heart. You are My little one, keep up your faith. Do not allow anything nor anyone to stop you. Give testimony that Jesus is the Son of the Living God, and always stand up for My holy Mother. I have chosen you, My poor little sinner, the greatest sinner of them all, because I do not always choose the best. You are an example of that nothingness that I serve whenever I please. You are the darnel that will become wheat. You will only give much fruit if you take refuge in Me, in My Divine Heart, and in the Immaculate Heart of My Mother. If you are now doubting, you will soon stop doubting. My Words have already been printed in your heart. I will not set you free yet from the chains that are holding you captive in this land, and you will still have to suffer because of Me. Always listen to My Words."

Mary speaks:

"Dear little son, my little one, I suffer with you, and daily I ask God to forgive your sins. They are many. If you knew how much God loves you, you would never sin again; if you knew how much my Son suffers for your sins, you would stop sinning. If you knew how much my Immaculate Heart suffers when you sin, you would not sin again. Keep steadfast in prayer, do not despair, and never reject the bitterness you feel at times, in your hearts. It is a grace from God that allows for your purification. Soon, your bitterness will turn to joy. Do not lose heart. Recite the Rosary daily, as I asked at Fatima, and at so many other places. The end of times draws near. You are living in the midst of the time of tribulation. The era of mercy is ending. Wretched are the inhabitants of the earth who only worry about gathering riches, or of crying out to heaven about injustices. I will soon run to the desert and you will remain alone with your faith. Faith alone will endure. It is necessary that it thus happen to fulfill John's writings. My entire celestial army serves you now. Do not waste one single day without doing something for your God. These are yet happy days, filled with graces, but chastisement is approaching for all.

'Do not store up for yourselves treasures on earth, where moth and decay destroy, and thieves break in and steal. But store up treasures in heaven, where neither moth nor decay destroy, nor thieves break in and steal. For where your treasure is, there also will your heart be.'[4]

I have been preparing you all of these years, to be the light of the world. Go, my little ones, and give testimony of your faith, let nothing stop you. My angels are preparing with you the path for the Lord's Second Coming. If you do not see me, it is because heaven so has planned it for you. You will soon see me, and you will see my Son coming down in glory and majesty from heaven. The Lord and your God, my Son Jesus, will remain with you until the end of times.

Endure it a little bit longer, be patient, you will soon see Him; He is at the threshhold. In heaven the uproar of the battle is already felt, and satan will soon fall into the depths of hell. The Archangel Michael will put chains on him, and you will be freed from his oppression. There is little time left; you will be persecuted and disturbed because of your faith. Some of you will be betrayed by relatives and friends, others will be shackled, and still others will die. Everything is written there. Do not put off for tomorrow what you can do today. Turn to your Lord and your God. Time draws to a close; the harvest is close at hand.

I bless you all, in the Name of the Father, of the Son, and of the Holy Spirit. Amen."

November 27, 1992 - *Feast of the Miraculous Medal*

Jesus Speaks

"Get up with the little breath you have left, and write, this is what the Spirit says to the churches:

'... to the angel of the church in Sardis, write this:...I know your works, that you have the reputation of being alive, but you are dead. Be watchful and strengthen what is left , which is going to die, for I have not found your works complete in the sight of my God.'[5]

My little son, if you knew how much I love you, you would do everything in your power to love Me. Listen to Me. At times My voice will sound distant, as if lost in the silence of your own conscience, and yet it is My voice. Allow the Spirit to guide you. Obey My teachings. Bow before My greatness, I am Jesus your Lord and God. You do well when you adore Me and kiss the ground as a sign of humility, and of submission. You would do better if you did not sin. Get up with the little breath you have left, and give yourself to Me. Look for your sure refuge within My Heart. Steered by My hand, you will not get lost. Open the door. I have been calling you for years. Do you recall the first time you read Revelation? You never thought that you would be granted the grace to live it all. We were always one. From the time you were a child, you belonged to Me. From many dangers I have saved you. How much has your guardian angel sustained! You named him Gallein, but his true name is Raphael. He is just as you imagine him to be. He is not very tall, and if you could see him, he looks like a 12-year old boy. He belongs to the warriors' choir, and is also an artist. It is he who wounds your heart with a spear, and lavishes you with tears that wash your soul and prepares you to receive My Mother and Myself. You are in the midst of your purification. Stay away from sin, and allow yourself to be guided. We are no longer two, but one. You are understanding more and more. Your road will not be easy, but is the road of the Cross an easy one?

The Church will undergo a horrific crisis, but it is you, My little ones, who are in charge of keeping its treasures and of safeguarding its teachings. It is not the physical, but the spiritual that matters. From the beginning of the world, everything has always belonged to Me. The fusion of heaven and earth is approaching, and everything will be renovated, made anew. When? It will come like lightning. Some will be taken, and others will be cast aside. What would happen, My little son, if I did not forewarn you of all this? Rest assured everything will take place as it has been written. This is the generation that has been chosen to live My Second Coming. This is the generation that has been chosen to suffer chastisement for its crimes and sins against heaven. This is the generation that has been chosen to test the ocean of My Mercy, and the zeal of My Justice. This is the generation where My Name will be engraved in the depth of people's hearts, molded like silver, and cast like gold. This is the generation that will not come to pass unless all that has been said by Me, and by My prophets before Me, has been accomplished. This is the generation where I will separate the darnel from the wheat, and where the darnel will be tied in bundles and thrown into the lake of boiling fire, and one third of it all will live forever. These are the last days. Repent, and turn towards Me, your Maker, your Lord and your God."

Mary Speaks:

"Dear and beloved little son of my heart: your heavenly Mother is speaking to you. Open and let me in. Oh, my little son! If you knew how it pleases me to watch you pray! This is a special day for me. I saved your life when you called me for the first time, asking me to wound your heart. I have been with you since then. I never abandon those who call upon me, or who implore my motherly protection. I am the Miraculous Virgin, Mother of Jesus, Mary of Nazareth. Today is a holiday for me, and I am close to all of the beloved children of my heart. Be happy and rejoice, for the Kingdom of God is at hand and my Son's Second Coming is at the threshhold. Prepare yourselves for the spiritual communion with my Son Jesus. Yes, children, many are the hours you must spend in prayer, and beside the Cross in order to see me. You must grow in the virtues I prize the most. Do not drive me away with your impurity or your arrogance. Be humble, listen to my voice, in the silence of your hearts. Open up to your brethren. I will always enlighten you with discernment. Last night it was your angel who pierced you with his spear, so that I could enter. I bless you and I comfort you in your moments of tribulation, of solitude and of silence.

Keep feeling less than nothing, because you are nothing. Only God is everything. I bless you in the Name of the Father, of the Son, and of the Holy Spirit."

November 27, 1992 (10:05 p.m.)

Mary Speaks:

"My little one, I have come to see you. I am your Mother, most blessed Mary, Immaculate Virgin. I have come to teach you about LOVE. You have spent your whole life-time in search of something that you do not know, because you were away from God. If you have not been able to be freed from sin, it is because you have not loved God as you should. In order to love, you must first be disposed to open your heart and follow your desire to look for Him. Once you open your door, He will enter, in rushing streams of fresh water that wash and purify you. Before falling asleep, tell Him that you invite Him in your sleep to keep you in His presence, and He will come to you and will fill you with His love. Upon awakening, tell Him, "Lord, I love you," and He will embrace you as a loving Father does, and will bless you all day. During the day, tell Him to keep you company, and He will be present in everything that you do; tell Him that you offer Him your tribulations when they arise, and He will fortify you. Tell Him that you need Him, and He will comfort you. Kiss and embrace His cross, as often as you can, and He will help you carry yours. Love Him as your best friend, each minute of your life, and He will be your best friend. He, my little son, is your Lord and your God, your loving Father, your Brother, and your best Friend. There is nothing on earth that He ignores. Ask His forgiveness for all the times when you have offended Him with your sins. Do you not realize where you have fallen? Ask for His forgiveness now, while you still have time. Ask anything from Him with love, and He will grant it, provided it does not hinder your soul's salvation. Whenever you embrace your children, parents, brothers or enemies, you are embracing Him and He returns it with love. When you look at the needs of abandoned people with love and with compassion, you are creating your path for your own forgiveness. It is all in the Our Father: '...Forgive us (our trespasses) and our offenses, as we forgive (those who trespass against us and) who offend us...' Yes, My little son, we must forgive all, so that He may forgive us; we must give it all away, so that He gives all away to us. Await everything from Him, and seek only Him. In time, your love will become more pure and more sincere if you listen to His voice. The opposite will happen if you become absorbed with material things; it will become harder for you to love. God will give you time for everything if you ask Him, but remember: accept the cross that He assigns to you; do not reject it. Difficult times for mankind are coming with no work and scarcity of food. Soon you will have to flee and hide in places where you cannot be found. My Immaculate Heart will be an unfailing refuge, and so will be the Sacred Heart of my Son, an unshakable fortress.

Yes, there will be events in heaven and on earth not yet seen: the howling of the seas, and the roaring of the earth will fuse with the whistling of the hurricane, all together forming a frightening noise. Soon many cities will disappear from the face of the earth, mountains will tumble, and the valleys will be covered with ashes. All will be wrapped in black smoke and many will suffocate to death. My poor children, how far you have fallen! In the end, My Immaculate Heart will triumph but before then, many will perish. The inhabitants of the earth will look at one another in total disbelief and many will denounce God. Those who remain will envy the dead. Look at those pale faces that resemble people coming out of their graves! How lonely will you be in those days, but remember, in the end, your freedom will be close at hand. Just a bit longer, and you will see the victory of My Immaculate Heart, and you will see my Son coming down from heaven in glory and majesty. Look, thousands and millions of angels are coming down to earth singing their praises. The Divine Light invades it all. Hearts are healed, tears dry up, the valleys come into bloom with remarkable magnificence, the City of Love will start its reign on earth. The Celestial Jerusalem, The One Without Blemish will welcome all those who remain alive. The Reign of Love and Life will have started. You will all be one, and God will rule in every heart. What has been foretold will be fulfilled: only one shepherd and one flock. Now I bless you, in the Name of the Father, and of the Son, and of the Holy Spirit, and remember: learn to practise love henceforth, otherwise you will not be able to live in the Celestial City that My Father has prepared for you since eternity. I love you very much, good-bye children, good-bye."

November 30, 1992 (6:00 p.m. approximately)

The Virgin Mary, Mary of Nazareth speaks:

"Yes, little son, you all are being told so many things, and you do not wish to understand. I have been at your side for a long time.

Soon, you will have me no more. There will be many who will invoke my name, but will not find me. I will be in the hearts of those who prepare a path of love. I have already said it: "I will write your names on small, white stones that only He will know where to find". That small stone represents each of your hearts, purified by pain, my children. I will be there with all those who welcomed me and my Son, during the time of mercy. I will be there with all those who testified that my Son is the Living God and the Ruler of Heaven. You will soon have to confront the beast and its followers from hell and bear witness with your deeds. Do not be afraid. My Son, Jesus, will put in your lips the words to be said, and the Spirit of God will seal your foreheads with the Divine Light.

Has it not been said that the Spirit will come over every flesh, and that the children of God will prophesy, will experience dreams and visions that not only enlighten their own paths, but that lead others to the Lord? Those shall be hours of loneliness and anguish for many who have forgotten God and me, while they still had the time. Do not be afraid. No one can steal heaven from you if you have prepared the way. God in His Infinite Mercy still gives you a few days. There is little time, and darkness covers all. You are the light in the midst of confusion. Evangelize all the peoples, heal the sick in the Name of Jesus, pray the Rosary, receive the sacraments while you still can. My Son is very lonely in the tabernacle; visit Him often and He will remember you when you are alone. Cry over your sins my children; I shall pick up every tear, and offer each one like a flower before the throne of the Lord.

Say with me: *'Mary, Mother of Mercy and of Comfort, we take refuge in Your Immaculate Heart.'* I am the safe ark that will take you to the Lord in the midst of the storm. I am the ark described in the Gospel of my Son Jesus. Invoke my name, and take refuge under my mantle that will protect all of you. Do not be worried any longer about the material world. The material is only useful when it can give glory to God. The more you accumulate, the more difficult it will be for you to let go in the near future. You are filling your hearts, meant for God, with the world of consumption.

Remember the First Commandment of the Lord's Law: 'You Shall Love the Lord Your God with All Your Heart, and with All Your Soul, and with All Your Mind. And You Shall Love Your Neighbor as Yourself.'

The physical world hardens so many people's hearts; they are no longer able to love their fellow men, much less God. Yes, children, the world of consumption has driven humanity to a lack of self-control, and to a coldness of heart. The Commandments of my Son Jesus, are no longer kept. The opposite occurs: Man invents his own, and lives them as he wills, without remembering God or his fellow man. How distant is he from the light and the truth! My enemy has managed to conquer many souls but I will save many others from his clutches, all those whose names were written in the Book of Life.

And now I give you my refuge and I bless you in the Name of the Father, and of the Son, and of the Holy Spirit, the Spirit of Love and of Consolation."

November 30, 1992 (12:05 p.m.)

(I have just prayed the Angelus).

Lord, a few days ago I had a dream that was divided into four continuous scenes. In the first scene, I saw a clear sky on a very starry night; one of the stars had four times the splendor of any of the others, including the celestial bodies surrounding it, and it was at the center of them all.

In the second scene I saw a clear sky but contrary to the first scene, only the big star appeared larger than before, close to half the size of the moon.

In the third scene, still night at approximately 3:00 a.m., I saw a very shiny light, as if it were the sun hidden behind some fog, yet there was neither fog nor sun.

In the fourth scene I saw a street, with some buildings and many people running in the background. I saw a woman with an anguished expression on her face at the lower left corner of the scene. I also saw some huge rocks falling from the sky into the street, and at that point I suddenly woke up.

Tell me, Lord, does it have something to do with what is coming?

The Lord speaks:

"Do not worry about what is to come. Everything is in My hands. It is written that the sky will crash against the earth and this will not only be an act of My Mercy, but of My Justice. If it were not for My directing all these things, mankind would end My creation much sooner than expected. Yes, heaven will interfere and My angels are prepared for the chastisement. They themselves shiver regarding this day."

Lord, I also hear a dull noise when I think about these things.

"It is the roaring of the rolling stone that is soon coming, and its curse will extend throughout the earth. It is why I am warning you that these times are serious, and that time is short. Turn to Me and to My most holy Mother, and take refuge in My Mercy. If man knew how much I love him, he would prostrate himself before his Creator. If he does not do so for love, he will soon have to prostrate himself wearied with pain. I will listen to whoever invokes My Mercy and will give him My Refuge, and I will be like a hen that protects its chicks. He who takes refuge in My Mercy will not perish."

Lord, make me humble; and may I receive what You will in prayer, that it may be truly an inspiration from the Holy Spirit. I am afraid Lord, afraid of making mistakes, that it may not be You speaking to me. Help me and forgive my doubts.

"I forgive you. How many times have I not forgiven you. Three times, three-hundred times, three-hundred-thousand times. Because I love you I must keep forgiving you. Perhaps you are not aware of how immense is My love for you?

I do not tire in forgiving those who implore My protection and My mercy, but I am a God of Justice as well, and I reject those who do not invoke Me with their hearts. I throw out the lukewarm. Love Me as you are, but love Me with all your heart, with all your strength, with all of your being, above all things. Let nothing or no one come between you and Me. Look for Me faithfully, do not lose heart, I am your Lord and your God.

Do not reject the dwelling I have prepared for you from all eternity, nor exchange it for things of this world. Let go of the earthly and look for the things of the Spirit. Following the example of My saints you will be able to see how they modeled themselves after the Divine Model. I found those who looked for Me and those given to Me I brought safely to the house of My Father."

Tell me, Lord, what must I do with this book?

"You must make it known when I tell you, provided that your spiritual director or priest who looks at it does not raise objections."

Lord, what would happen if one of them raised objections?

"Nothing. Everything has already been set in writing. No one can hinder the fulfillment of My Word. Everything will come to pass as it has been written."

Lord, does this dialogue tire You? I worry that my questions may bore You and that You leave me.

"No, I do not tire of your company, because I want you to love Me more and more. Little by little the flame of My love will set your heart on fire. My love will burn you. I am the God of Love. In Me alone will you be able to find the inexhaustible source to realize completely your thirst to love."

Lord, I had another dream. I saw a lady covered with a dark blue cloak which was full of stars. She stood next to a stone fountain and I could not see her face from where I was. As I approached her, she seemed to be playful and did not allow me to see her face.

"Yes, it was My Mother, the most blessed Virgin Mary. The fountain represents her as well, and the water symbolizes My Purity and My Word. She is the fountain keeper. If you wish to see her face, you must practice the virtue of purity. If you wish to drink from the fountain, you must keep My Commandments."

Lord, I am tired and long to rest. It is late at night, could You wait until morning?

"If you like I can, but love Me as well in your sleep. Love Me for the rest of your life. Your days have been counted from all eternity, and the time given you is to be used only in loving Me.

Rest, as you ask. I bless you, in the Name of the Father, of the Son, and of the Holy Spirit."

Thank you, Lord.

October 1, 1992 (7:55 a.m.)

December 1, 1992 (7:55 a.m.)

Good morning, Lord Jesus.

"Good morning, little son. What do you want to talk about today?"

Lord, talk to me about riches.

"Wealth was created for God, not God for wealth. The destiny of everything created was to give glory to God, but the devil rotted the tree of life from its very roots. By sinning, Adam and Eve lost the wealth of paradise. God created paradise to serve man and glorify God. It was part of God's wealth for man. Wealth was created for paradise, and not paradise for wealth.

The serpent reversed all of God's original plan and hence God, the Father Almighty, had to send Me, His only Son, to restore everything. As a second Adam I took that first man's place. My Mother, the most Blessed Virgin, took the place of that first woman and became the second Eve.

In His immense wealth, God gives man My greatest treasure, My Mother, the Virgin Mary, who in this way participates in My works of deliverance. Yes, from the onset, Mary, who is God's hidden treasure, is being prepared to be offered as an exalted fruit of the paradise that was lost by the serpent."

Lord, and what must man's attitude be regarding riches?

"The Gospel explains it all:

'No one can serve two masters. He will either hate one and love the other, or be devoted to one, and despise the other.'[6]

Wealth was created for man, not man created for riches. If all creation has been destined to glorify God, then wealth and man have been created to glorify God.

Look at Mary, My greatest treasure. In her humility, poverty and total submission, she glorified Me, who had been announced by the Angel Gabriel to be her Son, her Lord and her God.

My most blessed Mother possessed the greatest wealth when, by obediently giving Herself, She found God. And God possesses in Her, His greatest treasure, a living paradise where man will always find peace and rest, enabling him to assuage his thirst to love.

To amass riches is of no good to man if he neglects his relationship with God, and forgets his brothers. How many are there who, focusing on wealth, forget to gather the bread crusts left over from their tables to give to the poor? Truly I tell you,

> **'For it is easier for a camel to pass through the eye of a needle, than for a rich person to enter the kingdom of God.'**[7]

How many foolish women forget to light their lamps in time for the wedding that I have prepared for them, and instead waste their time in vainglory. How much wealth is squandered in giving way to arrogance, envy and the ego. How many riches are set aside for idolatrous ends, and wastefully consumed. Many exhibit wealth at their dinner tables, but the poor and hungry have less food than the dogs that lick their own wounds, at the entrance of chapels or of their own mansions. How much wealth is spent by those who boast of their power, convinced that the passing glory and comfort are useful in going to heaven.

I truly tell you that your Father who is in heaven, keeps an exact inventory of your wealth, and of how you use it.

Some people do not even pay the tithe established by My Church, to help them to cut down the weight of their sins, and to help in making God known. My Church performs many deeds of mercy through tithing. Other people neglect to give alms, thereby losing a powerful tool to wash so many sins.

How many innocent children are currently dying of hunger, and how many mothers have shrivelled breasts unable to nurse their infants at birth. There are hungry people, there are hungry cities, there are hungry countries. Soon, all of mankind will be hungry, but not because God created a world with limited wealth, but because man has mismanaged it with his egotism, and he has forsaken his brethren. If you only shared with the most needy one percent of what you store up in your dwellings, and in the banks where you keep your wealth, poverty would be eradicated. If you shared ten percent there would be real wealth, and if you shared 100% you would again be in paradise.

Soon My Sacred Heart will triumph and the Sacred Heart of My Mother, her most pure and Immaculate Heart will also be victorious. Then, a new reign of wealth will start, ruled by My Sacred Heart and by that of Mary. In that period which is imminent, the Church will be very poor, and the clergymen and bishops will walk barefoot; many of the faithful will consequently also walk barefoot. It will be a time of love and of joy, where all will share their bread like true Christians and all will return to truly worship God.

It will be a time of true riches, where the spiritual will have overcome the physical. Those of you who survive to the end will live in Celestial Jerusalem, in The One Without Blemish, in the City of Love, where sin has been put aside, and you will then be enlightened by My Glow. Love will flourish everywhere and all of My children, the ones who have a true devotion to Mary and to Me, will praise God and it will be the Reign of Charity, of true wealth. Surrender yourself if you want all. Give up all while you still have the time, because soon everything will be taken away from you. Then what will you be able to give, if you do not even have anything for yourself, much less have God with you?"

Lord, when I started writing this morning, I wrote October 1, and not December 1, why?

"On October 1, I had already given you the same message, but you had not known how to listen to Me. That day is the feast of Saint Theresa of the Child Jesus, such a beloved saint of My Heart, a virgin who found My riches. That day is the eve of the Feast of the Holy Angels, who are yet another sign of My great wealth offered to humanity. The voice of your conscience is nothing but the voice of the angel, whom I have assigned to walk before you, so that he edifies and points the path that takes you back to God. Be grateful to him and honor him for all his endeavors. He will be with you until the day you die.

If a man loses his soul, it is not his angel's fault but his own, for not having listened to his angel's voice. Those who are not conscious of their own sins, have pushed their angel away from them, and unless there is a special intervention of the Holy Spirit, it will be difficult for them to find the path. When you sin, your angel is present and keeps an account that will be displayed in God's kingdom the day you die. If it were not for Me, no one could be saved, and if it were not for My Mother, no one would come to Me. If you were conscious of your sin, you would not sin. God sees everything everywhere, and your angel is His faithful witness. Purge your sins, and follow My Mother's advice; receive the sacraments of Reconciliation and the Eucharist. When you have sinned, confess your faults to the priest who represents Me on earth. Do not look at his faults, but at your own. Receive Communion, the Eucharistic Bread as much as you can, and keep in the state of Grace, without mortal sin. Recite the Rosary, all 15 mysteries, daily. The Rosary is like flowers tendered before God's altar.

Be persistent in prayer. Persistence denotes faith; you will obtain many things through faith, and your prayers will be heard. I, your Lord and your God, endured until my death on the Cross. Practise My Ten Commandments of the Holy Law of God. They were given to man so that he would obey them. Those who change and modify My Commandments will go astray and will not see God. Be meek, and accept your mistakes. Be submissive, and humble yourselves before God, and before your brothers. Practise fasting. Fasting is a powerful weapon that purifies your soul, and God bestows gifts and graces through fasting. Fasting, along with prayer, charity, and the sacraments, forms the foundation and the path that lead to God. When you fast, do not allow anyone to notice. Dress and look your best. On that day give to the poor what you did not eat. Your heavenly Father will reward you in secret.

'But when you fast, anoint your head and wash your face, so that you may not appear to be fasting, except to your Father who is hidden. And your Father who sees what is hidden will repay you.'[8]

Now rest, little son, and I bless you in the Name of the Father, and of the Son, and of the Holy Spirit."

October 1, 1992 (3:40 p.m.)

December 1, 1992 (3:40 p.m.)

Lord, upon leaving the Holy Mass at noon, and coming back home, a question arose in my mind: Can You explain to me the difference between what an Apostle of the End Times is, as Mary requests us to be, and what does it mean to be a false prophet or a false Christ?

"Thank you, little son, for your question gives Me a way to clarify this to many. When I speak in the Spirit, I speak as God, in the very depths of your consciences. False prophets are those who invent things that have not been inspired by the Holy Spirit, but by the spirit of confusion and of chaos. How can you detect the Holy Spirit from the evil one? I have taught you, as Saint Paul said, that the Holy Spirit looks for Christians who accept their crosses.

'Many deceivers have gone into the world, those who do not acknowledge Jesus Christ as coming in the flesh. Such is the deceitful one and the antichrist.[9]

The false prophets are not moved by faith but by vanity and pride; they preach a different gospel to Mine, a gospel not based on love, but on egotism and on self-indulgence. This gospel denies the power of Christ Jesus and denies that Christ Jesus is the only Son of the Living God. It portrays Christ Jesus as just one more teacher of wisdom, denying that He is God and is the Second Person of the Most Holy Trinity.

Some false prophets deny that I am the Second Person of the Most Holy Trinity, and they call Me another saint; others simply ignore Me and still others say that I never existed, or that I was a myth formulated by mankind. Others deny My Mother, or the dogmas of faith defined by My Church; others contradict My clergymen and My bishops; others reject My Commandments, and My Gospel of Love; others repudiate their brethren, and by doing so they repudiate themselves; additionally, others are possessed by the evil spirit, whom they worship. Others destroy My Church on the surface; but those who injure it the most are the priests who, on many occasions, destroy My Church from the inside, leading many souls to their ruin by their example and their teachings.

All this sort of confusion and undoing is what false prophets are. The false Christs wish to parallel themselves to the Redeemer of humankind, and they forget that I am the Christ, the Savior of the human race who paid with My last drop of blood for you, and for your sins on Calvary.

Shortly, the prophet of the antichrist, under the direction of the beast, will invalidate the Eucharist. Churches will close, altars will be destroyed, and when this happens flee to the hills as it is written, because grief and loathing will have infiltrated the Temple of God. Today, the liturgy of My Holy Sacrifice is destroyed and once My Most Precious Blood is no longer offered to My Father in reparation for the sins of the world, the blood of the faithful will flow in the streets."

The Virgin Mary speaks:

"My dear little child, Jesus has explained to you who the false prophets are, and who the false teachers are. He has also spoken to you about the false Christs, but you wanted to know who the Apostles of the End Times are. My Son has allowed me to clarify it for you; from the time that I appeared in La Salette I have called on the Apostles of the End Times, on my true disciples of the Living God who reigns in heaven. The Gospel is already warning you that Christ Jesus will come from heaven in glory and majesty. Do not be confused, because that is why My Divine Son admonished you in the Gospel according to Saint Matthew (24):

**'If any one says to you then, "Look, here is the Mesiah!,"
or, "There He is!" do not believe it.'**[10]

Since my Son will come from heaven when the moment for His Second Coming arrives, and not even the angels know when this will take place.

What I can disclose to you is that His coming is approaching and that this generation will not go by without experiencing it. Be prepared because it will arrive like a thief in the night."

October 2, 1992

December 2, 1992

Most holy Mary speaks:

"Exult your God and worship only Him! Thank you my little child, for having heard my call. You did well in going to confession, because sin tarnishes your soul and distances you from your only Lord and God. When you went to receive the Holy Eucharist, I was already at your side and you were aware of my presence. I blessed you with my presence and helped you to cry for your sins. Your mission, my little child, is to rescue many souls.

I know that at times you resist in doing so, and you doubt about your assignment in life. Do not be afraid. I am with you. You voluntarily offered yourself at Peñablanca to work for me and I am leading you by my motherly hand.

Your own terrestrial mother prophesied in October of 1986, that you would become an apostle. I have heard her prayers, and yours. I repeat what I said in La Sallette: I call upon you my children, the Apostles of the End Times, who have persevered in prayer and sacrifice. You have offered yourselves to me. You are willing to immolate yourselves for my Son Jesus and you have been rejected by the world, or have left it in order to serve my Son Jesus and me. You have paid tribute and offered your cross to help my Son carry His; you suffer because of your brothers; and you keep struggling in silence. Each and all of you, who is pure and who participates in the battle against my enemy, is my apostle. All of you sinners, who are in search of me will soon find refuge under my cloak. I urgently call upon all of you, beloved and favored children of my heart, go forth and enlighten with the glow of Divine Wisdom so many of your brothers who do not know me yet, or who have forsaken my Son Jesus and me. Go, my little ones, and proclaim yourselves to be the Apostles of the End Times. For your entire lives, I have been preparing you for this unique plan: Your witnessing that my Son is the Son of the Living God, Ruler of Heaven, and that I am His most holy Mother.

Go forth, and announce the good news to your brothers throughout the world. The Second Coming of Christ Jesus is at hand, and you must be clean and without blemish in order to be selected by Him. If you sin, do not lose heart, get up again. Only a bit longer and you will see Him coming down, surrounded by choirs of angels. And you will also see Me next to Him, because I am His most loving Mother, and wherever my Son is, I am at His Side, loving and adoring Him for all eternity.

You are part of my small flock. I have prepared you during all these years so that when the division comes, you will be able to meet and support one another. You will need to get ready not only in a spiritual way, but also in a physical way. Use your resources wisely so that you may be prepared for the most difficult moments, and bear always in mind that what you have, you must share with your brothers who are most in need. Do not store away what you are not willingly able to share."

Why, my dear little Virgin, did you also make me write October 2, at the start of this message?

"My little son, October 2 is the date celebrated by the Church in honor of the Guardian Angels."

I open a book of saints, with the important Church festivities, and I read:

> ' No evil shall befall you, nor shall affliction come near your tent, For to his angels he has given command about you, that they guard you in all your ways.'[11]

> 'In the presence of the angels I will sing to you, my God.'[12]

I am the Universal Queen of all creation. My Son Jesus has crowned me and given me that title, and consequently I am the Queen of Angels and Mother of the Church. But, above all, I am the Immaculate Virgin,

Mary of Nazareth, Mother of Jesus and your Mother, the Coredemptrix, the Full of Grace, the Immaculate Heart of the Incarnate Son of God, Queen of Peace, Queen of Mercy, Mother of Consolation, and the Mediatrix of all Graces, God's Paradise, the Sealed Fountain, the Ark of the Covenant, the Burning Bramble, the Flame of Love, the Comfort of the Sick, the Light of the East, the Root of Jesse, Tower of Ivory, Queen of the Prophets, Queen of the Apostles, Mother Most Pure, Mother Most Prudent, Mystical Rose, Perfume of God, the Victorious One who will crush the head of the serpent.

Yes, children, I am she, whom God destined from eternity to be the head of the Celestial Army to conquer evil implanted by the serpent in the first woman (Eve,) and through Eve it was carried to all of mankind. Yes, my little children, I participate in that marvelous plan of God to redeem the human race, fulfilled with the sacrifice on Mount Calvary of my Son Jesus.

That is why I gave you the date of October 2. Love your angel, because he is a member of my Army in heaven and you another member of my Army on earth. Soon both heaven and earth will join and you will be able to meet your angel, united in singing praises to my Son and to myself. I bless you in the Name of the Father, of the Son, and of the Holy Spirit, Amen.

December 2, 1992

Jesus speaks:

"Dear son, do not doubt that I will come, and I will come soon. You will be rejected by many and will grieve but do not be afraid, because your agony will soon turn to joy. You will find yourself in the midst of the final battle. It will be the final event before My Second Advent.

Heed My warnings; be prepared and do not lose heart, because will the Lord still find faith on the face of the earth when He gets here?

Do not be foolish, prepare yourselves. Open the path with prayer and good example. Practise the works of Mercy and the Commandments of My Church. Obey the Commandments of the Holy Law of God. Be always in the state of Grace, and do not let night fall when you are in sin, or away from Me. Entrust yourselves constantly to your guardian angels, stay away from evil. Pray for those who offend you, for those who attack you and hurt you, for those who invite you to sin. Pray for the souls in Purgatory who are in most need of My Mercy; turn to, and invoke the saints; obey My most holy Mother Mary, recite the Rosary every day, and when you receive the Eucharistic Bread, do so as I have taught you.

Keep away from modern, superficial songs, that are not My true psalms. I ask women not to approach Communion dressed in a way that scandalizes people; I beg them to be submissive and obedient to their husbands, and that they live modestly and discreetly in these last days. Let them stay away from cosmetics and masks that imitate My enemy. I ask you all to change your television sets [the tube] for altars, where you worship only Me. My adversary, the old serpent, the devil or Satan, will be coming through the television screens as the Anti-christ himself; that is why you must keep away from the television that has a putrefying effect on you, since it transmits blasphemy and sin, staining and perverting your consciences as well as those of your children. Read in Revelation the fate awaiting those who welcome the sign of the beast's number on their hands, or on their foreheads, or to those who adore its statue or image. That is why I insist that you keep distant from television screens, because the very anti-christ, the incarnate devil will seduce many through this means. My poor children, how I suffer for you all.

Read Revelation 13, 16, and 14:9. I have instructed you too much, My little child, for you to remain silent. Already one hears the voices of those who deny that the End Times is approaching, claiming that the theories of the millenium have influenced the people who speak that way. My poor children, you do not know what you are saying. I am at the gateway, and I will shortly descend to you and many will say, "Lord, Lord," but they will be in the vestibule, not in the temple and will be left outside

'And throw this useless servant into the darkness outside, where there will be wailing and grinding of teeth.'[13]

Yes, children, come back to Me while there is still time for conversion and for turning back. Return after receiving the sacrament of Reconciliation with open, humble and pure hearts. Do not allow a single day to go by, without receiving Me in the Eucharistic Bread. OBEY MY POPE. My holy Mother has prepared this Pope for you, My favored Son as a model, and head of My Church, and I have confirmed him as My Unique Head and Representative on earth. Do not be deceived. Someone else will soon be coming to teach you a gospel different from the one I taught. At that point, return to the faith of your ancestors, and in your grandparents you will find the true faith. Today, faith no longer is found in your parents —fathers or mothers— and hence, I am asking you to bear your elderly in mind.

Saint Paul has already admonished you about this, and I confirm it to you. Yes, My children, the hour is serious, and accordingly it is compelling that all of you know about My warnings. This is why I ask you not to rest, day or night, until you finish this book because it will show many things that must be perceived in order to better endure these times.

Obeying My Pope, the true Pope, will guide you during these obscure days of your oppression. He who teaches a different gospel, or who changes My Commandments is not with Me. Look how My adversary has already seized many, and how they refuse and change the truth proclaimed by Me, in My only and true Gospel, in My Gospel of Love. Do not be misled. One of My chosen popes, Saint Pius V, had already established the liturgy for My Holy Sacrament of the Mass that should have been maintained until the last days, but the last Councils came about and the liturgy was altered. Submissive to My Church, I had to resign Myself to many outrages with said changes. Yes, I, Jesus, your Lord and your God, had to submit Myself to the decision of My ministers to give Me their backs; and to people giving Communion in the churches, without the sanctification of the Sacramental Order, nor having been instituted as deacons.

I have been humiliated, stepped on, massacred and denied by many, due to those new ceremonies. What pain do I feel when My children receive Me in their hands; what pain do I feel with a soul receiving Me without having been cleansed in the sacrament of Reconciliation.

They say, "I ask God to forgive me, and He forgives me," but they ignore that I founded a sacrament to be respected not by a few alone, but by all. Others say, "The Pope allows it" (they refer to receiving communion in their hands) but they forget or they do not know that even the Pope is coerced, and that he has been pressured to tolerate the requests made by many of My children, in order to avoid a greater partition within My Church. My poor children, how you have fallen!"

Lord, I must interrupt Your teachings for a few minutes, since I must pick up my little son from school.

"Do not be concerned. I will wait for you, I have always waited for you, go with My blessings in the Name of the Father, of the Son, and of the Holy Spirit."

October 2, 1992 (10:48 p.m.)

December 2, 1992 (10:48 p.m.)

Lord, here You have me again, I feel You still want to say something to me, please do so, if You wish. (I pray to the Holy Spirit).

I ask the Lord to speak to me through the Sacred Scriptures; opening my Bible, I read:

> 'Then he said to his disciples, "the days will come when you will long to see one of the days of the Son of Man, but you will not see it. There will be those who will say, Look, there he is [or] Look, here he is. Do not go off, do not run in pursuit. For just as lightning flashes and lights up the sky from one side to the other, so will the Son of Man be [in his day]. But first he must suffer greatly and be rejected by this generation. As it was in the days of Noah, so it will be in the days of the Son of Man; they were eating and drinking, marrying and giving in marriage up to the day that Noah entered the ark, and the flood came and destroyed it all. Similarly, as it was in the days of Lot; they were eating, drinking, buying, selling, planting, building; on the day that Lot left Sodom, fire and brimstone rained from the sky to

destroy them all. So it will be on the day the Son of Man is revealed."[14]

"Yes, children, that is why I ask you to be ready. If you decide to take a trip, you prepare your affairs, and advise your closest relative or friend, to entrust him with your business while you request that he keeps you informed if an accident occurs. What would you say if the trip you intend to take is to Eternal Life, and the only baggage allowed is the good deeds that you have performed here on earth? What better relative than My own Mother, who never neglects you and runs with interest to your side when you invoke Her motherly protection? My little children, do not disregard the matters concerning Me. If you dedicated at least one sixth of the day to prayer, you would enjoy more plentiful fruits and a more secure pathway. As I have said to you, it will be like in the days of Noah and many will be left out of the ark; and it will be like in the days of Lot, and many will perish. Accept My Mother as the Safe Ark, and listen to her messages. Do not be foolish because time is running out, and your deeds are not enough to merit heaven. The poor have already gained a portion of heaven while on earth, and so I am calling upon the rich and the powerful to share what they own with love. Of what use is it to have so much when it is not shared with love? Read Corinthians 1:13."

Lord, it is almost midnight and I need to sleep, I have not yet prayed my Rosary, I ask You for the conversion of X, and my own.

"Your prayers have already been heard, little son. Give thanks to God, and now I bless you in the Name of the Father, of the Son, and of the Holy Spirit."

THE SECOND COMMANDMENT:
'You Shall Not Take the Name of the
Lord, Your God, in Vain.'[15]

December 3, 1992 (9:17 a.m.)

Good morning, Lord, I have just returned from Mass and while in church, I was hearing many things, some coming from You, and others from Your most holy Mother. Could You repeat them?

"Good morning, little son. You did well to attend the Holy Sacrifice, and to receive the Eucharistic Bread. As I have already said, those who eat My Bread have Eternal Life. Well now, up to this point we have talked about the First Commandment of the Holy Law of God. Today, December 2, I will speak to you about the Second One, and so on, until we have completed the Ten Commandments.

The First Commandment embraces them all. People at times forget that the First Commandment is not only to love God above all things, but to assist the hungry, their brethren in the world.

Thus it is written: 'You will love the Lord your God with all your heart, with all your soul, with all your mind, and with all your strength. Love your neighbor as you love yourself.' I repeat all of this to you so that you understand the rest of the Commandments in reference to the First one.

As a child, you learned that the Second Commandment is *'thou shalt not use the name of God in vain.'*

You then thought that as long as you did not swear or promise anything using the name of God in vain, you would not commit sin. Oh, little son! If man knew how much he offends Me with his blasphemous jokes, discrediting My most Holy Name and that of My Mother. Satan mocks the virgins, and he undertakes to convince many innocent souls by this means, so that he can prepare them for sin. The Second Commandment is broken with disrespectful, mocking stories. How many other times is the Name of God used to trick in businesses, or to captivate the innocent? Another sort of blasphemy is to threaten someone **in** the Name of God.

Yes, little son, man has not meditated, and he has removed himself from My Commandments. My Mother has already warned you in many of her messages how, through radio, films, magazines, the press, and television both the black beast, and the beast with the appearance of a lamb (free masonry and the ecclesiastical free masonry infiltrated the inner circles of My Church) intend to destroy My Name, and the faith of My faithful.

How many curses the media throws out on a daily basis. If you listen attentively, you will become aware how every time you or your children turn on that rotten screen, the one you call television, [the tube] all kinds of insults, curses and blasphemies are spoken offending My Name, My Dignity, and the name of My Mother. Unfortunate are those who serve as a reason for scandal, for they would do better to tie a stone around their necks and throw themselves into the sea. I grieve for you and for your children, since the price due for purification of your sins will be high. Yes, little son, how many profane films are produced against My Name, against the Gospels, against My Mother, and against My Apostles?

You who work in the world of communications, open your eyes and wake up. You bear the weight of your sins because you have served as the keystone for scandal, bringing about the loss of so many of My children. You will pay for the blasphemy and slander that you have proclaimed. With your adulterous, violent propaganda you have cheapened My Commandments, and have sent many people to perdition. Meanwhile, you not only pride yourselves and design your names in gold letters, but you humiliate My most Holy Name.

Yes, little son, a just judgment awaits all of these people, on the day when I come to judge the living and the dead.

Is it not perhaps written in the Gospels, that the smallest word used vainly will be weighed, and that it will carry a price on Judgment Day?

Lord, forgive us our sins, many are ignorant and do not know what they do. Have mercy on us for having been so deceived. Where is Your Mercy? I feel no one, Lord, will be saved with what You are saying, because we have all sinned against Your Holy Name. Forgive us, Lord, have pity.

"Yes, little son, salvation is not an easy task but My Mercy is infinite. That is why from now on I am calling upon you. You are being warned for the last time. Whoever resorts to My Mercy during this period of My Return, will find the doors of My most holy Heart open, and will unite with Me, like a drop of water blends in the ocean. Yes, little son, I will forgive all sinners who plead My Mercy with a contrite heart, and with intentions to reform. This is the hour of My Mercy but woe to those who blaspheme against the Holy Spirit; those will not be absolved neither in heaven, nor on earth."

Lord, how else can one sin against the Second Commandment?

"Just as it has been written, My little son, the most frequent way to sin is by using My Name in unnecessary swearing, and by committing perjury in the courts of justice. Men swear that they will do this, and do that; country leaders pledge to carry out improvements that they are not able to accomplish; criminals swear their innocence when they are really at fault, and all of them forget that I have said,

'...and you will know the truth, and the truth will set you free.'[16]

Yes, little son, sinning against the Second Commandment leads many to violate the Seventh. They are not conscious of sinning, nor do they remember. Yes, little son, the devil roams the earth, and has unleashed his rage knowing that time is short."

Lord, thank You now, and for all Your teachings. Help me, Lord, to observe this Commandment.

"I have not yet finished, little son. How will you remember that I have cautioned you how people speak of what they carry in their hearts?

Learn to listen to what they say to you, and learn to detach yourself from those who blaspheme and insult, from those who curse and swear using My Name for anything. Try to correct the ignorant, but if they do not listen, ignore them and pray for them.

Today it is common for people to invoke the name of My enemy, of the devil, and of hell. They use it all the time. Do you believe, little son, that it will bring them blessings? Some of them blaspheme constantly, saying that they are children of satan, when they are My Children, disregarding that I created them, that I gave them life, and that through Baptism, you have been declared children of God in the Name of the Father, and of the Son, and of the Holy Spirit.

Yes, little son, on that marvelous day in the lives of many who call themselves Christians, you became a part of My Kingdom. What have you done with your Baptismal Seal? Some of you have ignored it, and some others have denied receiving it. How many parents are there who fail to baptize their children, refusing them these Graces? This, little son, is another way of breaking the Second Commandment since they say, "They are allowed to choose when they grow up." In this way they not only ignore My Name and My Power, but they take away from them My Grace, and the pathway to heaven.

And this is all for now, little son. I bless you in the Name of the Father, of the Son, and of the Holy Spirit."

Amen. Thank you, Lord.

THE THIRD COMMANDMENT:
Remember to Keep Holy the Lord's Day

Lord, I have just read the message dated December 2, to a friend, with whom I have shared this secret, and I have realized that the date is not 2 but 3. Why, Lord, have I made the same mistake?

"You have not made a mistake, since I have wanted it this way. Have you forgotten that I have asked you to write this book day and night, until you finish it? For Me the past, present or future do not exist. I **am** always everywhere. The Our Father teaches you to live one day at a time, and to ask God for your daily bread. Every time that you break a piece of bread, think that God is giving it to you for that day, thank Him and bless Him for His generosity.

Honor and glorify Me, your Lord and your God, in everything that you do. Now we have reached My Third Commandment, that is to comply with holy days.

Yes, little son, I am anxious for My messages to be disclosed, because they will point out the way for many people. You are only an instrument at My service. Without Me you would be nothing. Then, why did you ignore Me for so long? There are many people today who do not attend the Holy Sacrifice of the Mass. If they do, they mock My Body and My Blood; how then, do they expect to obtain pardon for their sins? Whoever abandons the Holy Sacrifice of the Mass rejects Me. Whoever substitutes other entertainment or pastime for the Sacrifice of the Mass is belittling Me at the foot of the Cross on Calvary. How many times have you not heard people say that to worship Me once a week is boring, or that they feel lazy and do not take time for the Mass since they consider other activities more worthwhile? How will I speak to these on Judgment Day, when they are expressing themselves this way? They ridiculed Me, ignored Me, and subsequently turned their backs on Me. I also will reject them, if they do not repent now, and if they do not humble themselves before their only Lord and God. Imagine that you are asking your children to attend your own wedding with Me, that is, on the day you die. While many of your friends and relatives gather together for the occasion, your children abandon you making merry, though you remain alone in death, in a freezing tomb.

If you knew their ingratitude, how would you feel? Yes, little son, whoever fails to honor the holy days, and does not attend the Holy Sacrifice of the Mass on Sundays, is ignoring Me and withdrawing from My Table. Oh, children, if you knew how I yearn to see you at the foot of My Calvary, or humbled at the foot of My altar asking Me to pardon your weaknesses! I wish to forgive you but for that, I need to have you come close to Me and acknowledge Me as first in your lives, before any diversion or subterfuge prepared by My enemy. How many substitute a car race or a fashion show for the Holy Sacrifice of the Mass? How many prefer to rest in bed, than to come see Me? I am alone in the tabernacles, My children, awaiting your visit. Not everyone understands the Sacrifice of the Mass, they think that I am not there, and that everything is a human misrepresentation to get your attention, and to receive alms. How wrong you are! Of all that I have left for you on earth, the most significant is the Sacrifice of the Mass. Nothing compares to the Sacrifice of Holy Mass. Upon blessing the bread in the Cenacle, I left you My Living Body, and the same happened with My own Blood. Yes, children, I am here, a real God waiting for you to receive Me. Many among you question where the idea of Sunday sprang and why it is not on Saturdays that you are to attend the Holy Mass that commemorates My Sacrifice on the Cross. It was Saint Peter who changed it from Saturday to Sunday, because this enabled many Jewish people to attend the Sacrifice. Many new converts and supporters of My Religion could not attend the Sacrifice because, as you know, the Mosaic Law prohibited them from walking long distances on Saturdays. Yes, children, the tradition of My Church was grounded in the truth; but there are already some who say that the truth was modified by tradition."

Lord, it is now lunch time, will You allow me to continue later on?

"Yes, little son, go with My Blessings in the Name of the Father, of the Son, and of the Holy Spirit."

Lord, here I am for You again, it is almost three o'clock in the afternoon. Do You wish to tell me something else?

"Yes, little son, I was waiting for you, thank you for being candid with Me, and with X. It is almost the Holy Hour of the day, the time when My Divine Heart opens for those who invoke Me and for those who love My Name. I am Jesus your Lord and your God, the One who died nailed to the Cross for your sins. Kiss the ground in sign of adoration."

(I kiss the ground).

"Yes, little son, embrace the Cross with love, or the Cross will embrace you. No one can avoid My Cross. Those who believe that they can escape from My Cross here on earth, will carry it in the other life. Never deny Purgatory, and never deny that hell exists. That is a deceit from My adversary to make you sin. I have not revealed anything new to you.

Everything has already been said, and consequently the Spirit speaks to the Churches: Whoever has ears ought to hear, and whoever has eyes ought to see. You need only to look and to listen in order to realize the time in which you are living, and all that has been said to you.

My Cross has been raised on the altars everywhere in the world, and My Blood has run from generation to generation to cleanse and purify you. It is because of this that I ask you not to miss the Holy Sacrifice of the Mass on Sundays, and to observe the feasts because I am He who redeems you from My Cross. I am He who redeems you when the priest, My favored son, pronounces the words that I taught in the Cenacle on the eve of My Passion."

"Do not trade Me for a little fun, cast aside your laziness and reach out to Me. Yes, children, one of the greatest obstacles for your spiritual growth is laziness, and it is one of the capital sins that bears down upon the whole world.

Lord, is there anything else that You wish to say to me?

"Yes, little son, during the Sacrifice of the Mass when the offertory basket passes by you, give generously. Do not give of your wealth, but of your poverty. Recall the passage in the Gospel, where a poor widow contributes with all she has to the Lord, while the rich man gives to show his action to the people, not to God. Always bestow generously without your right hand knowing what your left hand is doing.

You will be recompensed 101%, says the Gospel, and I promise you I will fulfill My Word."

Lord, without knowing why, I have left two sheets blank. Why?

"Yes, little son, I have left that space for you to set in writing and bigger letters, the formula used in transubstantiation. Do not forget it, because shortly someone will come who will attempt to change it, and accordingly prevent My Body from being immolated, and My Blood from flowing for you."

Lord, I do not feel worthy to write these words; besides, I looked them up in the Bible and could not find them. What should I do?

"Then ask a spiritual director that you choose to clearly write the formula for the consecration. Tell him to use the page on the left-hand side for the formula used in consecrating the bread, and on the right-hand side the formula used for the wine. He will understand, and the Holy Spirit will be upon him."

Thank you Lord, for so much bread. Tell me, my Jesus, have You also taught me that prayer?

"Yes, I was the one who revealed it to you. I bless you in the Name of the Father, and of the Son, and of the Holy Spirit."

THE FOURTH COMMANDMENT:
'Honor Your Father and Your Mother'

Good morning, Lord Jesus, I love you.

"Thank you, little son, for remembering what My Mother has taught you. I also love you. Did you already greet your father and mother, your brothers? Whoever greets his father and mother, is greeting Me; and who greets his brothers is greeting Me. Whoever loves his father, and mother, his brothers and his equals, is loving Me. And with this, little son, we have come to the Fourth Commandment of the Holy Law of God: Honor your father, and your mother.

How simple is this Commandment, yet how difficult for many to obey. Love for our neighbors is summarized in this commandment. There are many people who do not honor their parents, and consequently do not love them. Here is where man's ingratitude is measured. The Holy Family is the perfect model of love. Through it, you can perceive that indestructible triangle formed by a father, a mother, and a son. God gave you the Holy Family as a model of behavior when you live under the same roof. Look at Joseph's unselfishness and silence, My earthly father who was always tender and concerned about protecting and keeping watch over his family. How much Joseph had to endure; and his Seven Sorrows are remembered to this day.

Yes, children, the Seven Sorrows of My Mother parallel My own, and Joseph's Seven Sorrows are like those of My Mother.

Joseph was the skilled craftsman, descendant of kings, who knew how to accept the cross that God sent him. How I loved Joseph on earth, and how I love Him in heaven. His tears were united to those of My Mother, and together they prepared the way of My Cross. From them I learned to obey, and with them I exercised humility; not that I as God, would not know how to obey My Heavenly Father, but I had to live, as man, according to My Heavenly Father's plan, traced by Him from all eternity.

In Joseph, I found the good-natured father, always available, pure of heart, respectful towards My Mother, courageous in his silence, submissive in his work, strong in chastity, cheerful in the midst of tribulations, patient in waiting, obedient to his God, kind with his family, tactful with people, modest in taste, sincere of heart, loving with his family, self-denying in love, always available for My Mother and for Me, loving father, watchful as an eagle, and gentle as a lamb. Oh, Joseph, you know how I loved you on earth, and you know how joyous you felt when holding your God in your arms, covering Him with tender kisses. That is why today, you carry the name of Protector of My Church, and Family Custodian.

Yes, little son, commend yourself to Saint Joseph and be virtuous as he was, imitate his wisdom, his piety, his chastity, his love, his gentleness, his patience, his fortitude, his kindness and his obedience to the Commandments of My Law.

Yes, little son, now allow Me to talk to you about My Mother and about her relationship with Joseph and with Me. My Mother is the perfect model of earthly love. My Mother, a perfect model of virtues, was the absolute disciple of God. She learned everything from Him, and He gave Her everything.

Mary was compliant to Joseph and obeyed God, and she held the greatest mission entrusted to any woman, that of being the Mother of God. In My Mother I always found consolation, relaxation, silence, a total humility, and docility to My Heart. Oh, Mary, spotless mirror who reflected My Virtues, and in whom I could calm down my yearning to love. Mary, the Hidden Paradise of God, the Perfume of the Most High who always showed an ardent heart for God and for her people, glowing with the living, unquenchable flame of true love. Mary never hated anyone, not even the one who sold Me; on the contrary, She prayed for him and for his mother. Mary, the little one of God, the rest and support of her Family, nourishment for the love of God, unlimited gentleness, always readily watchful over her own people. Oh, Mary, how much comfort I found at your breast as a child, when you would caress My head and wipe away My tears. At home in Nazareth, I always smelled the subtle perfume emanating from My Mother's Immaculate body. The birds in the garden were aware of her kindness, and joyfully sang in her presence; many times the flowers opened at her passing. Mary was always prepared to follow Joseph and to watch over Her cherished Son. Mary was always solicitous with My apostles.

Yes, little son, that was My home. I never listened to harsh words; our hearts were always ready to accept the Will of God and to forgive.

We have arrived now at forgiveness. Yes, little son, forgiveness is a tool that God has given man to heal his wounds. Do you recall My words on the Cross?

Then Jesus said, 'Father, forgive them, they know not what they do.'[17]

How many parents are there who no longer forgive their children, and how many children are there who do not forgive their parents? There is no forgiveness among brothers, and parents do not know how to forgive one another either. Without forgiveness neither the heart, nor the spirit experiences healing. To forgive is heroic when forgiveness comes from the heart. It closes wounds that were open for years. It would be easier if people forgave the very moment the offense occurred. I have taught you to turn the other cheek to the person who hurts you, but you have forgotten this teaching.

How many children today feel resentment towards their parents and can never forgive them since they do not know how to forgive. They continue to live with the guilt of unforgiveness. How many marriages fail due to lack of forgiveness? How many children suffer the consequences because of parents who are unable to say, 'Forgive me for hurting you, because I did not know what I was doing.' How many innocent children, and how many destroyed families are there, due to a lack of forgiveness?

You have forgotten the easy path of forgiveness, that is TO PRAY for the transgessor. How often? The Gospel recommends 70 times seven. One of love's clearest expressions is forgiveness, without which your hearts will not heal. And your heavenly Father will not be able to forgive you. Remember the words in the Our Father...Forgive us (our trespasses) and our offenses, as we forgive (those who trespass against us and) who offend us...Yes, little son, forgiveness is in the nature of true love.

Many say, 'Lord, I do not love him, how can I forgive him?' They forget that the Fourth Commandment is also part of the First One, and that your duty is to love your neighbor, including your enemy. You must pray for your enemy, who is often no other than your own flesh. The person who hates his spouse, father or mother of his children, actually hates himself, and then how can he hope to enter the Kingdom of Heaven?

He who despises his brother, loathes his own blood, and hates himself. If you wish to obtain mercy, be merciful with your family; if you wish to be loved, learn to forgive. I instituted the family and it is indestructible. What does it matter that many of you appeal to judges, as in the time of Moses, to dissolve your bonds? This is to no avail. 'For what God has joined together, let no man put asunder.'

This is the law. Do not commit more outrages against your own flesh by unforgiveness. How much pride is hidden in couples who separate, because they do not know how to forgive! Yes, little son, remember that the devil is the king of contempt, and for that he fell into the boundless depths of hell. Do not allow the attachments of hatred to burden you any longer. Forgive one another, and thus you will be able to wipe off, with your own tears, the wounds that you have inflicted on each other. My poor children, where does My adversary keep you!"

Lord, I have not yet had breakfast and I feel hungry. Could You either wait for me, or come with me?

"Do you wish Me to accompany you?"

Yes, Lord Jesus, I want You to come with me, and together we will share this first meal of the day. You are the only family left for me. Will You bless my bread?

"Yes, little son, I will bless you, your bread, and your absent family as well, in the Name of the Father, of the Son, and of the Holy Spirit.

With this, My little son, we have come to the issue of abortion and of conjugal loyalty. My family at Nazareth was truly loyal. It was faithful to God before men, and each member was faithful to each other. We were united by trust, the human tie that stems from being loyal to God. A man and a woman faithful to God are moral, honest, and trustworthy. Trust is the thread that keeps the members linked together in a family life. When trust is destroyed, family life is destroyed. Trust can be regained through forgiveness. Yes, little son, My enemy has done away with trust in people's relationships.

The weapon used by My opponent that destroys the largest number of marriages is the sin of lust that we will consider further on. The evil spirit of lust attracts the members of a family with false perspectives of pleasure, of success, and of money detached from the family, driving the couple away from the true objectives of marriage which are to procreate children, and to raise them for heaven.

How many broken marriages are there because of lack of loyalty to God, and consequently to one another? Cheating is an appalling sin, because the demons of dishonesty and lust are hidden therein.

How many husbands abandon their wives and children seeking pleasure, and how many women covet disordered passions when cheating on their husbands? You roll about in mud. More than ever before, the serpent today invites women anew to excite men, and to attempt to destroy their family lives.

Women say, 'We have won a new position in the world, and now we have rights,' and they forget that while crying like this their children remain alone at home, substituting the motherly love they should be given, for the rotten television screen. Oh, foolish women of this century! Where have pride, disobedience, and arrogance taken you! The serpent will keep tempting you until the End Times, until it has finished with all of you.

Women: you have become conceited and cold hearted. Men no longer trust you, nor do they look at you as before. You have lost your place in your family lives, substituting them for worldly positions and their pleasures, and the results are paid by your children. Your wombs are left void, since many of you have spoiled your bodies in an attempt to avoid the birth of your children; many others among you have turned your husbands into useful eunuchs; and still others have become a source of scandal, changing the unconditional love that was your responsibility to give your partner, for some pleasure and wealth at the expense of other men.

Oh, foolish and arrogant women who run after your lovers; you will not catch up with them. You have prostituted yourselves and have drunk the wine of fornication, causing your husbands to look for comfort in other women. You are no longer the hidden treasure of which Solomon spoke, and have become like the woman of Hoseas before she was rescued from prostitution. Read Hoseas so that you may understand what I am saying.

Oh, women who offer yourselves to everything. The demon has stripped your bodies and has turned you into objects of temptation to attract men. You shock with your fashions, you daze with your movements, you overwhelm with your tastes, and you wear your hair in eccentric ways to call attention to yourselves. Your makeup has served to hide you from the truth of who you are, and your sensuality has deterred you from the path that you should follow as a family. This is the path which leads to heaven.

You have become defiant, cold and disobedient, and have offered your bodies to scandalize many. You are treated like queens so that you may be undressed, and thus you offend My Mother's decency; you are proclaimed executives, and thus you destroy your family lives. You have reversed the roles and have allowed My enemy to give you the status of men, and now you complain about what you have attained.

My poor daughters, you have ignored My Holy Family, and have been disobedient to My Commandments. Be submissive like My Mother and forgive your husbands, your children, and your own selves while there is still time; and you, husbands, follow the good example of your wives.

Yes, little son, I told you that we would speak about fidelity, and about abortion, but it was necessary before to also talk about trust, and about its connection with faithfulness.

Abortion, little son, is one of the most abominable sins against God, against your neighbor, and against yourselves.. My enemy directly attacks the First Commandment, the Fourth one, the Fifth one, and the Sixth one with abortion, in one single blow, and you, who have fallen to that unconsciousness and that coldness of heart, do not realize this.

The Fifth Commandment forbids you to kill, and the Sixth one to have intercourse out of wedlock. Abortion kills, and extends fornication, but it also commits a direct outrage against the love of God and against your own love of self. That is why now I will speak to you about abortion in the Fourth Commandment. Abortion destroys families in sudden ways.. Abortion is a mortal cancer that extends everywhere like a plague of the End Times.

Can a father trust a mother who has aborted one of her children? Can a mother trust again a father who has guided her to kill her son? Can a brother trust a sister who murders her heirs? Can a child trust a mother who kills his brother?

Yes, children, abortion turns members of a family, or an engaged couple, into accomplices of a crime that will not be easily forgotten. It has been said that God is only Mercy, and that My Mother teaches you that I forgive crimes. That is correct. But how many are capable of feeling in their hearts, the crimes they have committed? If they do not love their own children, how will they be able to love Me?

The love of God is shown in one of its purest forms in your own families. Your children are a sign of the creative power of God. God the Father is love. God the Son is love, and God the Holy Spirit is the Spirit of Love, the Comforter.

Yes, little son, with abortion you commit outrages against the love of God for you, and My enemy gathers My children at his ease. You, mothers who have aborted, offer Me in a Eucharist your unborn fruits. When you have baptized them from your hearts, I will receive your children and I will forgive you. Seek My Grace in the sacrament of Reconciliation and reform with the Eucharistic Bread. Have heart-felt remorse for the crime you have committed.

My Mother has already cautioned you that you have become worse than the beasts, because the latter ones watch over their offspring, while you murder yours in your own wombs; and not satisfied with your vanity, many grandmothers assault their own grandchildren by advising their daughters to abort.

If you could sense what those helpless, tiny bodies feel in your wombs that you have turned into death chambers, you would feel remorse forever. That is why the Gospel says,

'Woe to pregnant women and nursing mothers in those days.'[18]

The Ten Commandments

And somewhere else, you listen to your cries asking the mountains to cover you for the crimes you have committed against your own homes, against your own selves, and against God.

You have poisoned your children, you have butchered them, you have scandalized them and you have become pasture for the devil. Be humble again, and obedient like My Mother. Leave your crimes, your lovers, your egotism, your hatred, and your lust while there is still time.

Look, time is short. When My Justice comes you will be the first ones to be sorry. And now I bless you, My little child, in the Name of the Father, of the Son, and of the Holy Spirit, and may My Blessings remain with you all, and with your families. Little son, we have come, with this, to the Fifth Commandment."

But, Lord, what do You say to me about our relationships with relatives, employees, friends, enemies, etc.,.? Are they are not part of the Fourth Commandment?

"Yes, little son, but I have included them all in My First one, and in everything that I have said to you so far. Rest assured that if you follow the model of My Holy Family, everything will be granted to you, both in your relationships with your family and with your neighbors."

Thank You, Lord, for so much bread.

"Now rest, little son, and again I bless you in the Name of the Father, of the Son, and of the Holy Spirit."

Amen. Thank You, Lord.

December 4, 1992 (3:33 p.m.)

"And now, little son, let us talk about Christmas. I have left some room aside between the Fourth and the Fifth Commandments to speak to you about one of the most cherished holidays of My Father, of My Mother, and of the Holy Spirit Who, as Scriptures say, chose Mary for Spouse and is the Eternal love emerging between the Father and the

Son. Yes, little son, in that inscrutable mystery of One God in Three, Mary gives birth on Christmas Day to the Only Son of God. Through the Gospel you all know how I reduced Myself to the human condition, and with the humility of a one God, the world had a Redeemer. On Christmas day, little son, the three Churches (Militant, Suffering, and Triumphant) wear gala attire. My Mother, in many of Her apparitions on that day, wears a dress of spun gold; all the saints, and the heavenly angels sing hymns and psalms of praise, and the Triumphant Church is filled with joy and admiration before its Creator. Many graces are bestowed upon humanity by My Father, My Mother, and the Holy Spirit as He renders His Love.

On Christmas Day, many souls leave purgatory after their purification. Thanks to the Infinite Bounty and Mercy of My Father, they go up to heaven resplendent, and there the heavenly courts welcome them. On that day, My Mother obtains special favors for the three Churches. The Triumphant, Militant, and Suffering Churches unite in praise that goes up to the Throne of God as incense.

That is why, children, you must keep Christmas holy and prepare for the Spiritual Communion with God made man, in the very person of the Child Jesus.

On that day, My angels come down to earth and celebrate together with the families devoted to Me, one of My Heart's most cherished festivities. On that day God opens the doors of heaven for men of good will. Yes, My little child, do not profane Christmas with drunkenness and pagan practices, but instead celebrate My Birth with respect and love. That is the day of the most rejoicing in My Family, and on that day Joseph, my earthly father, blesses you as well filling you with graces. The Holy Family, always indestructible, emerges triumphant on Christmas Day.

Brotherly love must be felt by all. That is why I have chosen to speak about Christmas at this point. Do not mistreat your body, and do not kill the true Spirit of Christmas. Do not be excessive in material gifts, but remember the poor. Spend the day with Me close to the manger of Bethlehem, at the foot of the cave where a star marked the beginning of the Way of the Cross."

Thank you, Lord, for so much bread.

The Ten Commandments

THE FIFTH COMMANDMENT:
'You Shall Not Kill'

October 5, 1992 (9:54 a.m.)

December 5, 1992 (9:54 a.m.)

Good morning, Lord Jesus, I love you.

"Good morning, little son. I love you too."

Lord, last night I felt very bad, I felt very weak and my whole body ached. I felt summoned to accept Your Cross, but I was afraid. It is hard for me to suffer for others.

"Tell Me, little son, perhaps you did not offer Me your pain last night? What scares you? Last night I made you understand that the reward of Eternal Life is very big for whoever accepts My Cross and offers Me his, with all his heart.

And now let us talk about the Fifth Commandment of the Law of God, that is 'Thou Shalt not Kill'.

Yes, little son, this Commandment is in regard to those who kill the body, and to those who kill the spirit.

We have already spoken about abortion in the Fourth Commandment, about that monstrous war against the innocent where, in only ten years, the same number of lives as were lost in one of the major wars of this century, have been unnecessarily claimed. Yes, little son, the two world wars of this century account for less victims than the number of crimes committed through the practice of abortion, in this century. Satan has set up this abortion industry to destroy My Love.

That is why you have deserved chastisement and have prompted the Cup of the Rage of God to overflow. It is said in My Scriptures that before My Second Coming, you will see kingdom against kingdom, and nation against nation. Read the signs of the times. Many among you are afraid of the violence exploding everywhere. Yes, little son, you have turned the paradise that I gave you into disgraceful battle grounds, where neither peace nor security can be found.

This century is marked by violence and the demon of violence will steer you to chaos, and to your own destruction. You kill one another for everything, for a morsel of bread or for a bit of money, for material things, or because you disagree with one another. Scripture was fulfilled when My enemy possessed the spirit in Judas, and sold Me for a few coins. Many today sell their brothers, and many innocent, for a few coins. The devil named the place where Judas hanged himself, 'Bloody Grounds.' Yes, My little child, this hateful land was bought with the same 30 coins that desperate Judas returned to those who had paid him. Yes, children, today many men have become like Judas, killing and selling their brethren, and the demon has infiltrated the spirits of many who are preparing the sacrifice of mankind.

Do not keep participating in manslaughter, nor keep staining your hands with your brethren's blood, because in that way you do not store up treasures for Eternal Life, but rather build your dwelling-place in hell. Stop being insensitive. Through violence, you will only have achieved slavery and destruction. Yes, little son, the demon will manage to destroy many bodies; the dead among these who have kept My Commandments will see Eternal Life.

Up to now, little son, we have talked about those who kill the body with weapons ever more monstrous, and for increasingly less valid reasons. But what do you say about those who kill the spirit? My poor children, how far you have fallen! With alcohol and other drugs not only do you destroy your own bodies, but your spirits as well. Possessed by the demon of lust, humanity has uncontrollably succumbed in great numbers to the use of alcohol and of other drugs. You have been poisoned by your own hunger, thereby killing your bodies and weakening your spirits. You have become an easy prey for My enemy, who has twisted your outlook on truth, on reality, and has driven you away from Me.

Return while there is still time. Pray for drug addicts and if you happen to be one of them, yield yourself to Me, who will bring life back to you. Remember the words of the Gospel,

'...but he said to me, "My grace is sufficient for you, for power is made perfect in weakness."[19]

Accept your defects and willingly take that first step towards your salvation. Then seek Me, place yourself in My hands, and I will show you the way.

Jesus said to him, 'I am the Way, the Truth, and the Life.'[20]

My scourging atoned for many sins against nature, sins of lust, of greed and of desire for power.

Yes, little son, many sins are committed by you without realizing it. Tobacco is one of the most powerful drugs that slowly destroys you. You are ever more distant from the love that you owe to yourselves when you allow the smoke of satan, that already covers the earth, to seduce you to him. Return while there is still time!"

October 5, 1992 (3:03 p.m.)

December 5, 1992 (3:03 p.m.)

Lord, You know the pain I experience all over my body and the discomfort surrounding me. I feel weak and unwilling to write, yet I feel You still wish to speak to me about many things.

"Yes, little son, offer Me your cross, and write. There are those who not only sin against their own nature, but against My Creation; and by doing so, they are guilty. All those who kill My Creation go against nature, and against their brothers, risking the lives of others and their own. Yes, children, you have poisoned the waters, you have destroyed the forests, you have polluted the seas, and you have not even thought of your own future, nor the future of your children. You have thoughtlessly robbed the land with your feverish need to consume and consequently have forgotten your brothers.

You have exchanged life for death and a bit of money, which will soon be useless to you. You have turned the earth into a desert, the oceans into sewers, and you have filled the skies with satan's smoke and venom.

For not having been responsible, nor kept love in your minds, you have broken the Fifth Commandment. And there is still more. What do you say, little son, about those who slander and discredit other people? Whoever demeans his neighbor murders him. You embarrass people for any reason, and for the pettiest of things.

The apostle James cautioned you about this; you must learn to supress your tongues, for they sometimes wound more than the sword. Many wives today humiliate their husbands, and many husbands humiliate their wives. By doing this you forget that you are belittling yourselves and your children. Oh, My little child, all crimes weigh heavily upon this generation; ask for forgiveness and forgive each other, while the time for pardon and mercy is still here.

Yes, little son, those who belittle others are trying to destroy their brothers' dignity, and they make them unhappy by casting a shadow over their spirits. Do not worry because when I arrive as the Just Judge, I will wipe their tears and the slanderers will remain out of My House."

Lord, I am tired, is that all? At times I think that You are telling me so many things, that they will not fit in this book.

"Do not worry, little son, write; everything has been foreseen; keep offering your cross to Me today.

There are other ways of breaking the Fifth Commandment that are also included in the First, and the Third: all those who give their lives to My enemy end up by killing their spirits and lose Eternal Life. Understand, little son, that the spirit is indestructible. The followers of My enemy, who will soon receive a mark on their right hand or on their forehead, or those who will worship the statue of the beast or its image, will be chastised with the undiluted wine from the Cup of God's Rage. They will endure the torments of fire and sulfur; the smoke from their torments will rise up in front of the angels for ever and ever, and these souls will not find rest day or night.

Yes, little son, I am a jealous God; read Revelation (Rev. 13:16; 14:9,) it is all written therein.

There is so much that I have told you, little son, that you cannot remain silent. Among those who have given themselves to the devil are magicians, sorcerers, inventors of the horoscope, and all those who form part of the body of the black beast, masonry and ecclesiastical masonry that already constructs a false Christ, and a forged Church.

Soon the statue of the beast will appear before you, a powerful and oppressive idol that will threaten to death anyone who does not allow the mark to go on the hand or the forehead, or whoever does not worship its image or the statue of the beast. Yes, children, the time of your affliction draws near, and soon you will see the prophet of My enemy and the demon himself taking human form among you. Everything will come to pass as it has been foretold. One of My Mother's favorite children, and My own, has already cautioned you about all this.

In 1998 the veil of the mystery of immorality will be uncovered; the demon will be represented by the antichrist himself, and his reign will bring a lot of misery upon the earth. That is why I do not tire to call you to be prepared. All of you have been called to the road of Calvary, of martyrdom, and of the cross; but do not worry because a crown of glory awaits you in eternal life. Do not fear those who kill the body, as that is all they can do. Be afraid of those who kill the Spirit.

Keep away from evil books, from music where My adversary's name is yelled (rock) and from any other sort of idolatry, since all of that kills the Spirit and keeps you away from eternal life. I have already spoken to you about the harm produced by television. Stay away from it also, and do not go to discotheques or places of amusement where My Commandments are mocked. These places have become satanic churches."

Now, Lord, I wish to rest.

"Yes, little son, rest since with this we have reached the Sixth Commandment. I bless you in the Name of the Father, and of the Son, and of the Holy Spirit."

October 5, 1992 (8:45 p.m.)

December 5, 1992 (8:45 p.m.)

Lord, here You have me again, a bit confused. I thought that gluttony, and all of the false philosophies and theologies brought from the

Orient which oppose your one, true Gospel were also part of the Fifth Commandment. Gluttony kills the body, and these false teachings kill the Spirit.

"Thank you little son, I was awaiting your statement and it serves to remind you that we talked about gluttony already, when I explained the First Commandment. Of course, gluttony is included in the Fifth one, but the objective of having mentioned it in the First is for you to recollect that all My Commandments are included in the First one: 'Thy shalt love the Lord, thy God, with thy whole heart, and thy whole soul, and with thy whole mind. And thou shalt love thy neighbor as thyself.'

That will be the question that you will be asked on Judgment Day: 'Little son, have you loved?' In what concerns the false teachings that kill the Spirit, they also fit in this Commandment, but we will discuss them in the Seventh one."

Thank You, Lord. Tell me, why do You sometimes make me write two dates at once?

"The reason, little son, is to remind you that days shorten before My Second Coming. It also shows you the urgency of My appeal to spread My Messages, so that many souls obtain salvation. The time given for conversion is about to end. Due to the prayers of many people and because of the elect, the days of tribulation will be shortened. Yes, little son, pray and sacrifice."

Thank You, Lord, now I say good-bye to You, good night, cover me with Your Love during my sleep.

"Good night, little son, and now I bless you in the Name of the Father, of the Son, and of the Holy Spirit."

THE SIXTH COMMANDMENT:
You Shall Not Commit Adultery

Good morning, Lord Jesus, I love You, I trust in You.

"Good morning, little son, I love you too. You do well to trust in Me. And now let us talk about the Sixth Commandment, the one that people break the most, and the one that leads the highest number of souls to hell.

The Sixth Commandment teaches not to commit adultery. But there are already many who do not even know the meaning of that term. When you were a child, you learned that everything is important regarding the Sixth Commandment. Impurity is like a container, where everything that falls into it becomes infected and corrupt. Satan, the old serpent, is master of impurities.

I have already told you in the Gospel:

> **'But I say to you, everyone who looks at a woman with lust has already committed adultery with her in his heart.'**[21]

One thing is to yearn for a bond blessed by God, and a very different one is to desire a woman as a result of passion induced by the demon of impurities and of eroticism.

Today, man commits sins against the Sixth Commandment with all his senses, but his sight is the one faculty that leads more souls to perdition. Yes, children, you have corrupted your consciences by ignoring what you see. How many innocents absorb today that filth from birth. Through the media, the press, and films, you have made sex a daily nourishment.

Sex in itself is not evil; it was created by Me as a means, not as an end. Marriage is made holy with My blessings, and sex within marriage is a means through which the spouses share their bodies in the love of God. Sex expresses that love of God, and it must be regarded as such; this is why abusing sex outside of marriage, or in solitary acts, removes you from Me, and you fall into the hands of the demon of impurities.

Whatever you see filters deep into your consciences, like mud sits on the bottom of a container. When the water is stirred you become confused, and cannot see clearly. It becomes more difficult for you to distinguish good from evil; that is what my adversary plans, in order to lead you to perdition.

You are immoral in your thoughts, your words, your deeds, your omissions, and when you fail to give good counsel, or when you do not accept your children's daily imperfections.

You lack strength in refraining from sin. St. Paul teaches you that all sin is outside the body, but not sex and impure sins, for they remain within you, and in your consciences, causing you to violate your own bodies, and destroying you from the inside out.

'Avoid immorality. Every other sin a person commits is outside the body, but the immoral person sins against his own body.'[22]

You were taught that,

...Have you not read that from the beginning the Creator made them male and female and said, '...and the two shall become one flesh?'[23]

I am talking here about the spouses bound by the sacrament of Marriage. Any other sexual relationship out of wedlock is sin. Do not excuse your sins because you say there is love between you, or because you feel attracted towards someone. Do not confuse sex for love, nor love for attraction.

Love is an act of determination, and as such it must be carried out. That is why you are commanded to love your enemy. How many times is your own spouse not your enemy? What is it that you in truth do? Do you pray for the one who has lost his way? Do you forgive him? Do you seek him with love? No! What many of you often do is leave him, and find someone else who can give you increasing satisfaction. You forsake true love that you are asked to practise until you die; you forget about the loyalty you swore to one another; and you allow your passion to dominate you. You prostitute yourselves in any extramarital act. Yes, little son, this generation has become filthy with its own crimes; impurity causes more souls to go to hell than any other sin.

You have been made temples of the Holy Spirit, but you have flooded your temples with the wine of fornication demeaning your bodies so that Asmodeo[24] can conquer them. Remember when I chased the merchants out of the temple? And what is it that you are doing with your own temples?

The day you see the Wrath of my Father, He will also throw you out where there will be weeping and gnashing of teeth and your bodies will not be buried, but will become like manure covering the earth.

The Angel of the first plague has already been turned loose, marking those of you who have yielded to the pleasures of the flesh. He wounds the flesh open with ulcers that never heal. Plagues have developed because of your sins. Today you do not speak of marriage, but of 'relationships' and with this word you justify your filthiness and your lust. How many innocent are witnessing impure relationships among adults, outside of marriage?

Silly parents, come back while there is time! Stop sinning. It will not be easy for you, because satan has deceived you with his cunning, and while he is suggesting comfortable and pleasant lifestyles, he is preparing room in hell for you. Adulterous generation! How many among you have destroyed your brothers' marriages, and how many others, through your persistence and deeds prevent some spouses from reuniting, while you attach yourselves like malignant growths in the lives of those who do not belong to you?

Yes, little son, satan has taken many of you as his own, and unless you receive special graces from the Holy Spirit, you will be lost forever. I do not tire in calling you, keep away from your adulterous relationships and do not excuse them, pretending they are love.

Yes, little son, practise chastity in whatever state of life Grace finds you. Keep pure in your marriages, if you are married, and make an agreement with your mate. Days of continence in your marriage are a fasting that rises like incense to the Throne of the Lord, and He blesses you. Keep spotless out of marriage if you are single, and stay away from isolated acts of impurity.

Be chaste during your engagement, recalling the words of Saint Paul, that it is better to marry than to have an impure relationship.

> **'...but if they cannot exercise self-control they should marry, for it is better to marry than to be on fire.'**[25]

Yes, little son, and now let us talk about fashions. Many things are included in this area, not only clothing, but accessories, music, and false advertisements. Women's bodies have become lures and are used for pleasure. Satan causes sin through dress that seeks to assail the senses. He also inspires women to dress like men, and men to dress like women. The demon, the old serpent, wanted from the beginning of My Creation to cause confusion, and has wanted to destroy what I have made.

God created man with one set of traits, and woman as his companion so as to support one another, not to be baffled by their sex identity. Read Genesis. Man and woman were both created as such. The demon in his cleverness has managed to distort your sexual identities (unisex). Distance yourselves from trends that confuse your sexual identity.

Fruits of all this chaos are not only the increase in sensuality, but homosexuality, lesbianism, and all those doctrines and cults that direct you to worship your bodies, rather than to seek God and save your spirits. Women have accepted seduction, and by losing their place in the family have become vicious, and an instrument of sin and of pleasure. Just as the serpent seduced the first woman, in these latter days it invites you to sample the forbidden fruit that guides you to perdition. The price of Redemption has been very high. Return to Me. I will forgive whoever seeks My Mercy, as I did the Prodigal Son. Remember that parable, as well as how I pardoned Mary Magdalene. As penance, she was asked to sin no more; that is why she is a saint, and is among the heavenly court. Return to Me, while you still can.

It is written that before the End Times, and before the reign of My adversary, many of you will be denied the Gift of the Holy Spirit that allows you to differentiate good from evil. Today, you confuse ugliness

for beauty, licentiousness for freedom, impurity for purity, lies for the truth, discrimination for fairness, hatred for love, and hell for heaven. Justice is a fruit of peace, beauty is a fruit of truth, goodness is a fruit of justice. Love is a gift of the Holy Spirit that produces forgiveness.
Love a pure heart and become like children again. Repent from your immorality and confess your faults. Live in the holy fear of God, and I will receive you.

'...Blessed are the clean of heart, for they will see God...'"[26]

Thank You, Lord Jesus, it is hard for me to write, and at times I think that I have invented all this and that it is not worth the effort.

"Thank you for being honest with Me, little son. I will reflect on your words, and the truth will become clear. Do not be afraid, it is My adversary who tempts you and makes you doubt. And now, I bless you in the Name of the Father, of the Son, and of the Holy Spirit."

Amen, thank You, Lord, for so much bread. This time I am the one who does not wish to say good-bye, because there is something troubling me, and that You have not mentioned. Lord. You have not spoken to me about modern dances.

"Oh, little son! you are beginning to understand. You are refining your conscience. Your senses are all stimulated by music and fashion. Those two instruments are a powerful weapon used by My enemy in some dances. I had not forgotten this, little son, because I forget nothing. I am pleased that you are interested in My call, and that you are reflecting on My words. Yes, little son, many times some dances foment sin, and the body indulges in its desires and passions freely. Not all dances are evil. Stay away from those where the serpent takes possession of your bodies and you become its agents.
And now I bless you in the Name of the Father, of the Son, and of the Holy Spirit."

Lord, thank You, everything is now clear. What do You think of my visiting father X today, and of telling him about this book?

"If you wish. I will be with you. Go with God, little son, and now rest. In the Name of the Father, of the Son, and of the Holy Spirit."

October 6, 1992 (5:07 p.m.)

December 6, 1992 (5:07 p.m.)

Lord, talk to me about the witnesses that are named in Revelation.

"Yes, little son, the Book of Revelation talks about the coming of Enoch and Elias, who will evangelize full of the Holy Spirit. The Spirit of Enoch can be found in all those who evangelize and who follow My Commandments; and the Spirit of Elias is found in all those who welcome My Mother and support Her teachings. Yes, little son, when the Holy Family fled to Egypt, it sought refuge in the same cave that had served as a dwelling to Elias.

Due to blessings from My Mother, recently a church has been constructed there to recall the visions had by one My saints, Simon Stock. From that site the Holy Scapulary has been given to the world as protection against hell.

Yes, children, the Spirits of Enoch and of Elias can already be found among many of you, and they proclaim the assured triumph of My Sacred Heart, and that of the Immaculate Heart of My Mother. As I have already said to you, they announce the triumph of the Two Hearts and the defeat of satan, since at the End Times the doors of hell will not prevail against My Church.

You will soon see Enoch and Elias proclaiming the Word, and they will guide you during the difficult days of your affliction. At the end they will die but, after three and a half days, they will come back to life. (Read Revelation 11.)"

Why is it Lord, that sometimes You do not direct me to where I am to find the information that You give me?

"Little son, do not be upset, you must learn to seek.

'For everyone who asks, receives; and the one who seeks, finds; and to the one who knocks, the door will be opened.'"[27]

Thank You, Lord, for so much bread.

"Now I bless you, little son, in the Name of the Father, of the Son, and of the Holy Spirit."

THE SEVENTH COMMANDMENT:
You Shall Not Steal

October 6 (5:40 p.m.)

October 7 (2:47 p.m.)

December 7 (2:47 p.m.)

"Yes, little son, write 'time is short.'"

Lord, forgive me for not writing any more yesterday, I was exhausted.

"Do not be upset, little son. I know how to wait. Now write:

There are those who rob the body of what belongs to the body, and those who rob the soul of what belongs to the soul. If those who steal do not repent, confess their faults and return what they have stolen, or make compensation for their wrongs, they will not see the Kingdom of God either. Little son, it is necessary to replace what has been stolen. Many are indeed sorry and do not restore what was taken; so, by not being aware of the evil that they have done, they keep stealing.

What a shame, little son, that those who have possessions steal from those who lack them, and the same occurs when the needy steal from the rich thinking that this is correct. You have forgotten that I said to you,

> **'Ask and it will be given to you; seek and you will find...'[28]**

Children, you have become confused, for one who robs to accumulate riches will not be happy since what he has stolen will be taken from him, and he will be left naked, if not in this life, in the next. Your Father who is in heaven sees everything, and He knows what you are doing. Remember that even the last hair in your head is counted by the Father.

He who robs from the rich is not happy either, because by doing so he challenges My heavenly Father's kindness, forgetting the promises that I made to you in what is known as the 'Sermon on the Mount':

> **'Blessed are the poor in spirit, for theirs is the kingdom of heaven.**
> **Blessed are they who mourn, for they will be comforted.**
> **Blessed are the meek, for they will inherit the land.**
> **Blessed are they who hunger and thirst for righteousness, for they will be satisfied.**
> **Blessed are the merciful, for they will be shown mercy.**
> **Blessed are the clean of heart, for they will see God.**
> **Blessed are they who are persecuted for the sake of righteousness, for theirs is the kingdom of heaven.**[29]**'**

Prepare yourselves, while there is still time; return what you have stolen, and if you do not find the person from whom you stole, give it to the poor. Much suffering awaits those who snatch away what does not belong to them, and fail to return it. Do not follow their example and so deserve the same fate.

Look, My body was sold for only 30 pieces of silver and My temple is full of thieves. What have you done with My dwelling? Today, leaders steal from their governments, and the governments rob the people who, in turn, in order to justify themselves rob the governments. The rich never have enough, neither do the poor. You have abandoned prayer, children, and you have ceased appealing to your Father in heaven. In the end He will hear the prayers of the just, of the merciful, and of those who persevere.

He who is able to give to his brethren and refuses to do so, robs just as much as the poor who steal, for the latter sin by their lack of faith, handing over the heaven that they had already been bestowed here on earth.

Humbly accept the circumstances in which God placed you on earth, and do not worry about whether you are rich or poor. Care about the matters of the Spirit, living as God commands you.

Those who accumulate riches at the expense of their brothers, illegally taking possession of their goods, will sin against justice and they will be severely judged. Remember the good thief bound to the cross, he entreated My Mercy; he offered Me his pains with sincere love. Now, naked on the cross, I was his last refuge, and I accepted him with love.

Yes, little son, nothing will remain hidden; those who are now illustrious will be unmasked and their riches will crumble.

What use is it for an administrator to amass wealth on earth, if he goes before His Father empty-handed? John the Baptist already called you 'a race of vipers,' and I repeat this, you are like sepulchers that conceal the decay of your souls.

Now, little son, allow Me to speak to you about those who rob the Spirit. Yes, today there are many who, because of their desire for money, have set up enterprises that take away peace and purity of heart from many. Peace and purity are destroyed by businesses that cater to violence and sexuality. Belief in God and in humanity is destroyed. Through false teachings, true faith is lost and there are already many of My priests who are spreading evil, and without realizing it, many times worship My adversary.

But woe to those who openly abandon the true faith and set up a false temple bearing My Name. Freemasonry has imprisoned many of My children and these will have more difficulty in coming back to Me since they have consecrated themselves to My enemy and the devil is jealous of his own. I will help all those who summon My Holy Name with their hearts.

Repeat with Me three times: *'Blessed and Praised be the God of Israel, May He be forever blessed and praised. Jesus, I trust in You; and You, Mary, be my consolation and my salvation.'*

Thank you, little son, pray for all those who steal from you and who insult you; and remember the words of the Our Father,

' ... and forgive us our debts (our offenses,) as we forgive our debtors... (those who offend us)'[30]

Yes, little son, I include here those who rob the Spirit so that you become aware that he who sins against the First Commandment through idolatry, is also sinning against the Seventh. With the increase of these false doctrines the Eighth Commandment is likewise violated.

Yes, little son, sinning against one of My Commandments brings about consequences that you do not even imagine. Remember that Gospel teaching that if a soul once it is cleansed does not keep alert and in prayer, the evil spirit leaves it for awhile, goes to the desert, and returns to that soul with seven other spirits, so that the soul is in worse condition than before.

Pray and do penance, and enrich yourselves with your good deeds, not with your thefts and with your injustices.

And now I bless you, little son, in the Name of the Father, of the Son, and of the Holy Spirit."

Amen, Lord, thank You for so much bread. Lord, there are many things going through my mind and that You have not yet mentioned. Why?

"Thank you, little son, for raising these questions. Your conscience is being refined. The Gospel is full of examples that can relate to the Seventh Commandment of the Law of God. The parable of the rich man and Lazarus is one of them, but I also told you,

> **'If your hand causes you to sin, cut it off. It is better for you to enter into life maimed than with two hands to go into Gehenna, into the unquenchable fire. And if your foot causes you to sin, cut it off. It is better for you to enter into life crippled than with two feet to be thrown into Gehenna. And if your eye causes you to sin, pluck it out. Better for you to enter into the kingdom of God with one eye than with two eyes to be thrown into Gehenna...'[31]**

And now, little son, go in peace and I bless you in the Name of the Father, of the Son, and of the Holy Spirit."

Amen. Thank You, Lord Jesus, now everything is clear. Lord, I have yet another question. Is there anything wrong with having money?

"Oh, little son, what patience must I have with you, but at the same time I like your questioning since I am your God, your friend and your brother. No, little son, there is nothing wrong with having money if it is considered a means, but you should never esteem it as an end in itself. You cannot serve two masters at once, God and money, just as you cannot confuse what belongs to God, and what belongs to Caesar. Today you are confused, children, and it is why you see My priests involved in politics and in making money. They have displaced Me for power and wordly riches.

In La Salette My Mother warned you and I admonish you: Woe to those of My children who only concern themselves with valuing riches on earth, and who attempt crimes against My Justice; woe to those who only fret about attaining power. A sword hangs over their heads; in a short while it will fall upon them.

Come back while there is still time. And now, I bless you in the Name of the Father, of the Son, and of the Holy Spirit."

December 7, 1992 (11:40 p.m.)

"Beloved, little son of my heart, I am your most holy Mother, Mary of Nazareth, the Immaculate Virgin, the one conceived without blemish or sin. I am the Immaculate Conception, the slave of the Lord, His most holy Mother, the one assumed into heaven. Yes, little son, God has always been with me and He has appointed me as the Mediatrix of all Graces, and as your intercessor.

I am Coredemptrix since the very moment of my Immaculate Conception; from the time my heavenly Father prepared me to be the Immaculate Container, to give my own blood to my Son Jesus. Yes, little son, the blood of the Immaculate Virgin is the Blood of my Son the Redeemer of the world. Thus, when His Blood is shed, I too, am in each drop of Blood.

Yes, little son, where the Mother is, there is also the Son; and where the Son is, there is also the Mother. Jesus is not only the fruit of my womb, but I am also a fruit of God's Mercy for all of my children. I am the Mother of the Church, the Spouse of the Holy Spirit, the Mother of the Son, and the Heavenly Father's beloved Daughter. I am the Queen of the Universe, of all of creation and thus I love you so, my children. You have been made in the image and likeness of God, of the Second Person of the Most Holy Trinity, of My Son Jesus. I am the Pleading Omnipotence, the Mother of Good Counsel, the Health of the Sick, and the Aid of all Christians, the Refuge of the Needy, and the Queen of your hearts.

Give me your hearts on this feast of mine so that I will return them to you, pure and full of my love. Allow my maternal hand to soften you, and allow me to guide you to heaven. I am the Star that will direct you to the Lord. And now rest, little son, and I bless you in the Name of the Father, of the Son, and of the Holy Spirit.

Pray for the priests, little son, pray for all those who are in such need of prayers. Repeat with Me: *'Lord, give us holy priests and lay-people committed to Your Church, who are willing to follow the road of the Cross.'"*

December 8, 1992 (7:30 a.m.)

Mary Speaks:

"Good morning, little son, I am your most holy Mother, the Immaculate Conception, Light of the Morning, Pure Star of Dawn. Look how the fields are covered with my whiteness and are filled with my blessings.

Yes, little son, God gave me to you so that I may illuminate your souls and fill you with love, so that you may endure the remaining days. Announce without ceasing that I am the Coredemptrix and the Mediatrix of all Graces. These two truths are inseparable and intertwine, they will enlighten the dark days of your persecution.

Today I am with you like an eternal flame of fire. I wish to ignite my Love for God in you. Spend your time with God and with me in the peace of your hearts. Today the heavenly angels praise me and I appear to mankind as the Immaculate or White Rose, always ready to sacrifice myself for my Son, Jesus.

Be pure of heart, children, if you wish to please me and see me one day. Be humble and obedient. With these three virtues you will be able to open your path to heaven, a path that no one will be able to steal from you. Oh, little son, if you knew how many of you fill my Immaculate Heart with thorns. You are made for love, and love is nothing but total abandonment to God. Do not fear, because a golden crown awaits you in Eternal Life.

And now, little son, I bless you in the Name of the Father, of the Son, and of the Holy Spirit."

Jesus Speaks:

"Good morning, little son, I am Jesus of Nazareth, the Son of Mary, the Redeemer of the World. My Mother is the Immaculate Virgin, the bud that burns with love for God, who ignites you all with her flame of love for Me. If you knew how much I love Mary, there would not be enough pages to describe it, nor human time to tell of My Love. If you knew how much Mary loves you, you would want to die today to keep her company for all of Eternity.

Yes, little son, My mother is endless kindness and a secure refuge for all of you. Follow her light and if you do, with her you will not perish. My Mother is an inscrutable reservoir of sweetness, and her tenderness embraces all of you. Oh, little son, how I love those who love My Mother. She is the most powerful instrument that you have to reach Me, and to obtain whatever you ask of Me. I will grant you whatever you ask through My Mother's intercession, as long as it does not harm the salvation of your souls.

Remember well, My Mother is the Immaculate Conception, always Virgin, Mother of God and taken up to heaven, Coredemptrix and Mediatrix of all graces, Mother of the Church and your Mother.

Do not be misled, because the enemy will soon harm you, but do not fear; with My Mother you have a sure shield with which I have gifted all of you, Christians of the End Times. She, along with Me are your last resources. Wear the scapular and take permanent refuge in My Sacred Heart and in that of My Mother. Ask for your protection under her mantle; let it be your refuge. Allow her to prepare you in her Immaculate Heart as an offering to Me. Yes, children, your liberation is near."

THE EIGHTH COMMANDMENT:
'You Shall Not Bear False Witness Against Your Neighbor.'[32]

"Yes, little son, many sins are committed daily against this Commandment, that I have already told you is related to the others. Today, everybody lies for any reason, and truth has been confused with falsehood. The world of consumption has perverted you, and a free economy of consumption has distorted your minds. You cheat on the prices and in that way you not only violate the Seventh Commandment, but the Eighth one as well.

You lie in your business affairs, in your marriages, in your occupations, and you also lie by being careless."

How can you lie by being careless, Lord?

"Carelessness, little son, is the fruit of pride and of daring. The rash person pretends to give an image of himself that is not true. Not having high standards he confuses with his ways of talking and of behaving, thus creating chaos among his brothers; this chaos is produced by making false statements and by lying.

By being careless you also violate charity and the Love of God, and consequently you break the First Commandment. Wisdom is the mother of all virtues, and lack of it is the deepest root of all your sins.

Look at My Mother, the Virgin Most Wise; in her you have an unfailing model of excellence. She radiates truth, and surpasses all virtues.

Yes, little son, do not mistake discernment with half-truths. The latter are lies. Only the whole truth, and nothing but the truth will set you free. Half-truths are chains that lead you to other kinds of sin. With false witness, little son, many times you break the Second Commandment, and as I told you before, when you break any of My Commandments, you are breaking the First one.

You often dishonor others through lying, and in this way you break the Fifth Commandment that says 'You shall not kill'.

Your lying and giving false witness show what you store in your hearts; you destroy many and fill your brothers with sadness.

Lying leads you to fornication, to committing crimes, to stealing or to dishonoring your family and your brothers.

Yes, children, run away from lies that are an easy path to hell; from an early age teach your children to live in the truth, and the truth will set them free. Raise them with lies and you will enslave them to My enemy. False teachings and philosophies are also a sin against the Eighth Commandment. I had already mentioned this to you when I spoke about the Seventh, and its relation to the First.

Yes, little son, you must learn My Commandments in order to use them as a sure guide. Whoever does not know My Commandments does not know Me, whoever denies them, denies Me, and who does not follow them, does not love Me. To love Me means that you always observe My Commandments."

THE NINTH COMMANDMENT:
'You Shall Not Covet Your Neighbor's Wife...'[33]

"And now, if you wish, let us talk about the Ninth Commandment of the Holy Law of God, that is 'You Shall Not Covet Your Neighbor's Wife.'

Yes, little son, this Commandment was given not only to men but also to women. Today it is violated equally by both men and women, who appear to be like beasts in heat. They no longer unite in the sacrament of Marriage, as ordained by God, but unite under a judge who pretends to legitimize any union of concupiscence.

You no longer look for God's blessings to sanctify all, but instead try to accommodate His Holy Law to satisfy your human cravings, and weaknesses. You have turned your homes into stables, and your mates into cattle. Whenever you want, you push aside the Law of God to give into your carnal desires. In this way you have made your hearts censers of the demon.

I have already warned you in My Gospel that,

'... every one who looks at a woman with lust has already committed adultery with her in his heart.'[34]

Anyone who does this is guilty. I can say the same to women. I gave you these teachings when I spoke about the family, in the Fourth Commandment and when I spoke about adultery and fornication in the Sixth. Sex is only licit within the sacrament of Marriage, established by My Church. I have told you not to confuse sexual desires with love, nor love with attractions. Read in the Sixth Commandment what I have already taught you, in order for you to better understand the Ninth.

I am not a God of sex, but a God of Love. Sex is only an expression of God, a means and not an end, that sanctifies the sacrament of Marriage in true union with God.

And with this, little son, we have come to the Tenth Commandment of the Holy Law of God which is not to covet your neighbor's goods."

THE TENTH COMMANDMENT:

'You Shall Not Covet Your Neighbor's Goods: You Shall not desire your Neighbor's House, His Field, or His Manservant, or His Maidservant, or His Ox, or His Ass, or Anything that is Your Neighbor's.' [35]

"Yes, little son, and this is why I want you to end this book at this time, if it is possible for you. I will help you if you look for Me. Write, little son:

Covetousness is an inspiration that comes from the demon of envy and of lust. Greed is a double-edged tool that opens the appetite of those who are not satisfied, of the lustful ones, and of the envious ones, of those who are away from God and who do not accept the share that God gave them on earth, in order to reach heaven.

And those who behave in like manner, in excess, never calm their appetites and are always wanting more. They become insatiable beasts that find nourishment in the wastes, in the left-overs of injustice, and in their brothers' unhappiness.

Yes, children, where there is covetousness, envy is always present, and where there is envy, jealousy abounds. With this latter perversion of your feelings, you fall into an abyss that is difficult to exit. The demon is always ready to use his many subleties to deceive you; jealousy is but one step away from rage and from desperation.

How many desperate or enraged souls deny God and rebuke their brothers, and of these what a great number of them take their own lives or that of their kin. Yes, little son, the chain of sins belongs to the devil and it is a strong one that you alone cannot break. Come to Me, Jesus of Nazareth, the Meek One, the Good One, the Pure of Heart Who resembles you in all, except in sin. Yes, little son, I am the Son of the Living God, Ruler of Heaven, Who has come to you to set you free from your afflictions, and to offer you eternal life.

Trust in My Mercy. Say along with Me, *'Jesus, I trust in You; Jesus, I abandon myself to You; Jesus, I count upon You for everything.'*

And last, little son, remember that obedience is a precious key to enter heaven. Obey My Commandments and if you fall, get up again. I am always willing to forgive you if you come to Me with sincere contrition.

Remember what you learned as a child in cathechism. Before going to sleep, examine your conscience. Do not ever go to sleep in mortal sin, and if you have sinned make a sincere Act of Contrition, and go to a priest as soon as it is possible for you to confess your faults. Make a determined effort not to sin again. I know that you are human and I know how imperfect you are, but if you come and present your naked soul to Me, I will heal you and embrace you with Love.

Remember, little son, difficult times are close at hand, and it will be increasingly difficult for you to find a priest who is willing to listen. Dark days will come when absolution will be given to masses of people since it will be impossible for My ministers to hear individual confessions: this is why I call you now to be always prepared, and to acquire the habit of obeying My Commandments.

You have been given everything, little son, so carry it out. Open your hearts as the time of Your God is drawing near, and when I come I will be a Just Judge. I **AM** Who I **AM**, Who Was, and Who Will Be, the Alpha and the Omega, the Beginning and the End. Amen."

December 12, 1992 (10:55 a.m.)

My Lord, my God, and my All, Jesus of my heart, I am sad today because You know how hard it has been for me to pray all day, and how the enemy has attacked me. Tell me, Jesus, were You with me? At times I feel I can no longer bear it.

"Yes, little son, I am always with you, but it is you who is not always with Me. Today you were too worried about the material things and My enemy took advantage of it to try to hurt you so that you would fall into his trap. You did the right thing by not denying Me or by not rejecting your cross. Believe Me, little son, it serves you much more to offer it to Me, than to try to get rid of it. That is all for today, little son,

I know that you are tired, but you must remain alert as My Mother wishes to speak to you."

"Good evening, little son, I am your Mother, Mary of Nazareth. I love you and I bless you. Today is also a great day for me. I know that you remembered me this morning and I have been at your side all day. You forgot to invoke me when you were in most need of me, but later you remembered and I ran solicitous to your assistance.

Yes, little son, it has been 461 years on the 12th of December of 1531, that I appeared in Tepeyac Hill, to someone like you, whose name was Juan Diego. He was modest, little son, and that is why I chose him. You are all the opposite, little son, and I wish to teach you how to be like Juan Diego. Be meek and trust me. I am your most holy Mother, who does not abandon you. I know what you have done on my behalf and because of it you are with me. I will not abandon you, little son. You are mine, and in spite of my enemy's fury because you are in open battle to stay away from sin, I will be helping you and supporting you not only when you are succeessful but when you are afflicted.

You have lost your composure today, little son, and you must not allow it to happen because whenever you do, you go backwards in your climbing to heaven. Do not be afraid however, because I was with you all day. If any time you find yourself carrying a cross that you do not understand, do not question it. Accept it and remember that God's ways are impenetrable to men.

And now I bless you, in the Name of the Father, of the Son, and of the Holy Spirit."

Amen. Thank You, Jesus, and Mary, for so much bread.

December 19, 1992 (10:45 a.m.)

Good morning, Lord Jesus.

"Good morning, little son. I have been waiting for you all these days. Why have you abandoned Me? These are times of prayer and of recollection, and you have been worrying about material goods. Come back to Me, to My Sacred Heart, and to the Immaculate Heart of My

Mother, and take refuge there with your family. Days shorten and soon material goods will be a thing of the past. This is one of the last times when the inhabitants of the earth still have the opportunity to gather as families at Christmas time in the midst of affection and of joy.

Difficult days are to come, when there will not be any partying or gift-giving, and you will have to celebrate Christmas hidden within your hearts. Many of the families will have broken up and will suffer. In those days do not be afraid and take refuge in My Heart, and in the Heart of My most holy Mother. They will be a secure refuge and will lighten the way of hope, with their flames of love. In the end all will be renewed."

My Jesus, I have to ask a question in regard to this book. First: why, Lord, when the priest was about to set in writing on the left-hand page the formula as You requested, for the Consecration of the Bread, he could not because he only remembered it in Latin, and not in Spanish? After writing the formula for the Consecration of the Wine he no longer remembered it in Latin, and wrote it in Spanish. Yet, at the end he inverted the order and had to use numerals to keep it duly organized. Later, he remembered the Consecration of the Bread in Spanish, and wrote it below the one that he had written in Latin. In my humble opinion, he is a good Jesuit priest and has been celebrating Mass, according to what he said, daily for 20 years. What happened to him here? Please explain it to me, Lord Jesus.

"Yes, little son, he is a good priest and his intentions are good. He loves My Mother as few of them do, and has served to lighten the ways for many. What has happened is what I have allowed, to show you how the demon confuses many and how subtly and decisively has the black beast, the ecclesiastical masonry, infiltrated the inner circles of My Church. It will be vanquished in the end because the gates of hell will not prevail against Her.

The Council insisted on using Latin as a language whenever possible; yet, many of My ministers no longer speak it. This was the first step to demolish the universality of the Liturgy, and the importance of My House with its seat in Rome.

Yes, little son, the first step to demolish My Church was to change the Liturgy established by Saint Pius V, one of My chosen children. When the priest whom I sent you to, forgot Spanish, and then Latin, it was to show you today's confusion in the world. This confusion relates to the languages and the words which My priests use in consecrating, if they do not pronounce them correctly.

This is Babel, little son, chaos in the languages within the Liturgy. If the words that I taught are changed, or the order of the words are changed, there is no transubstantiation and therefore My Body is not consecrated, and My Blood is not shed.

When My Blood stops being shed on the altars, the blood of the faithful will run in the streets.

Yes, little son, with the Protestant Reformation My Body and My Blood ceased being shed and consecrated for many, and a great number of them died with terrible consequences for their souls. Soon someone will come trying to change it all. Do not listen to him. Soon a statue will be constructed to be worshipped by all. Do not worship it, because it is My enemy's statue, the antichrist, the demon made flesh.

Do not concern yourselves if you are imprisoned and taken before the courts of justice because of My Name. The Holy Spirit will inspire you with what you are to say. Do not be afraid if you need to face death, for a golden crown awaits you in eternal life. (Read Revelation 13, 16, and 14:9)"

Lord, and what do You tell me about kidnapping as it relates to the Fifth Commandment?

"Thank you, little son, for your question. When I spoke to you about the Fifth Commandment, I mentioned the kidnappings. Kidnappings are hateful crimes before God, and those who kidnap behave like Judas, looking for rewards at the expense of the blood and of the sufferings of their brothers.

I urgently call upon those who are kidnapping so that they turn their eyes to God, while there is still time. Eternal life is the reward for those who obey My Commandments, and hell is reserved for those who ignore them.

And now I bless you, in the Name of the Father, of the Son, and of the Holy Spirit, Amen. It is urgent that you have this book published, little son, it goes with My Blessings and it will serve as light for many. I will show you the way."

Amen. Thank You, Lord, for so much bread.

REFERENCES

Hartdegen, S. J. (1986) *The New American Bible for Catholics.* Canada: World Catholic Press.

Interdicasterial Commission for the *Catechism of the Catholic Church* (1994). Citta del Vaticano: Libreria Editrice Vaticana.

Whealon, J.F. (1975) *The Vatican II Weekday Missal.* Boston: Daughters of St. Paul.

The Ten Commandments

NOTES:

1 Matthew 4:10
2 Matthew 22:39
3 Matthew 25:42-44
4 Matthew 6:19-21
5 Revelation 3:1-3
6 Matthew 6:24
7 Luke 18:25
8 Matthew 6:17-18
9 2 John 1:7
10 Matthew 24:23
11 Psalm 91:10-11
12 Psalm 91
13 Matthew 25:30
14 Luke 17:22-30
15 Ex 20:7; Deut 5:11
16 John 8:32
17 Luke 23:34
18 John 24:19
19 2 Corinthians 12:9
20 John 14:6
21 Matthew 5:28
22 1 Corinthians 6:18
23 Matthew 19:4-5
24 name of a demon mentioned in the Book of Tobit.
25 1 Corinthians 7:9
26 Matthew 5:8
27 John 7:8
28 Matthew 7:7
29 Matthew 5:3-12
30 Matthew 6:12

[31] Mark 9:43-47
[32] Ex 20:16; cf. Deut 5:20
[33] Ex 20:17
[34] Matthew 5:28
[35] Ex 20:17; Deut 5:21